At
Home
In
Ireland

Picnic in a ruin
in the rain

At Home In Ireland

Cooking and Entertaining with Ava Astaire McKenzie

Ava Astaire McKenzie

FOREWORD BY Maureen O'Hara

ROBERTS RINEHART PUBLISHERS

*For my father and my Aunt Dellie for many wonderful reasons.
And because they brought me to Ireland.*

All photographs are by Ava Astaire McKenzie except for the following:
Front cover, pp. 58 (right and bottom), 104 (top) courtesy of Dick De Neut;
pp. i, 1, 5, 24, 32, 128 (top left) and back cover courtesy of Richard McKenzie;
pp. 49, 58 (left), 59 courtesy of Marcia Mitchell

Published by ROBERTS RINEHART PUBLISHERS
6309 Monarch Park Place, Niwot, Colorado 80503
TEL 303.652.2685   FAX 303.652.2689

Distributed to the trade in the U.S. and Canada by Publishers Group West

Published in Ireland and the U.K. by
ROBERTS RINEHART PUBLISHERS
Trinity House, Charleston Road, Dublin 6, Ireland

Copyright © 1998 Ava Astaire McKenzie
Design: Ann W. Douden

International Standard Book Number 1-57098-204-X
Library of Congress Catalog Card Number 97-76206
10 9 8 7 6 5 4 3 2 1
Printed in Hong Kong through Phoenix Offset, Ltd.

CONTENTS

A carrot is a carrot – a head of cabbage is a head of cabbage!
Ah no, not so, when they pass through the hands and the kitchen
of Ava Astaire McKenzie.

Ava is a gardener by fate, a fisherwoman by location, and a cook
by love. I think she got most of her magic from the leprechauns
who haunt her garden, her rockeries and her pools, and from the
wee folk and the fairy people who spy on her every day hoping
she'll leave a few "leftovers" for them. But there are rarely any
leftovers – just satisfied, happy, satiated guests. Add to all this
the fragrance of her floral arrangements and the imaginative,
artistic beauty of her romantic table settings. They are a
pleasure to behold.

Her husband Richard was finally able to persuade her to capture
between the covers of a book the wonders of her kitchen and her
table settings and their happy life together in Ireland.

So here you have it. Enjoy it and try to capture a little of Ava's
magic in your own kitchen and at your own table.

Maureen O'Hara

ACKNOWLEDGMENTS

Many, many thanks to the O'Regan family and all our neighbors for their friendship and help through the years: to Jeanne, Marcia, Brother Angelo and De Neut for spotting and fixing all my mistakes; to Mark and Joan for multitudes of computer rescues; and to my Richard.

A NOTE ABOUT MEASUREMENTS

All of the recipes use American measurements.
Use the conversion tables on page 148 to convert American measures
into Irish/British or metric equivalents.

Of Cabbages

Heather and rowan berries

(Facing) Ava in her garden

& Things

When you live in a place as beautiful as Ireland, you are certain to have many visitors, and, until they visit, friends from our Beverly Hills days usually don't believe that we live as simply as we've said, so we love to make them dig potatoes, gather mussels, and do the other country things which are so much a part of our daily routine. I guess their skepticism is understandable. Our life was a lot different then.

Bobby Short, one friend from those days, still shakes his head in disbelief whenever I talk about growing vegetables. Having been a mainstay at New York's Carlyle Hotel for over three decades, Bobby is the undisputed king of cabaret but, although we have been friends for years, it wasn't until we settled into this bucolic lifestyle with its proximity to Europe that we could accept an invitation to spend a few days with him at his house in the south of France each summer. Bobby probably didn't mean it to be every summer but he keeps inviting, we keep accepting. For three or four days we are part of his whirlwind social activities on the Riviera and always return home not quite believing it happened.

One such evening we were thrilled as Jessye Norman sang under the stars in the courtyard of the palace in Monaco, and when we found we were sitting directly in front of Prince Rainier, I remembered that I'd been worrying about the carrot crop with Timmy O'Regan at our garden gate that same morning. After the concert, we had supper with Jessye on a hotel rooftop where, fortunately, my fair knowledge of French helped me. Except for Bobby and Jessye and us, no one else at the table spoke English. There have been dinners with Joan Collins, Jack Nicholson, and Andrew Lloyd-Webber among

the cast of players at the estate Texas socialite Lynn Wyatt takes every summer, and at the home of our old friend, Roger Moore. At one smaller luncheon at the Marchesa de Riencourt's beautiful house, Prince Albert was seated at Richard's table. They obviously had hit it off well and I asked my husband to introduce me to his new friend, "Al," because my father had once dated his mother.

Apart from those few silly times with Bobby each year, our summer days revolve mainly around the garden, which we leave with reluctance. Occasionally at a fancy villa on the continent when people ask about our life in Ireland, I know that, because of my heritage and the sort of life they lead, they probably think we raise horses, or when I say I cook and garden, they assume I have a cook and point to things in the garden. Due to its size now, we indeed do require helpers a couple of times a week, but there is more than enough work for all of us. We have to – and like to do a lot of the upkeeping on our own. It wouldn't be any fun otherwise.

In this countryside, addresses are by name or townland rather than numbers and we thought our place's name, "Clonlea," was more suited to a grand manor house than a farmland cottage until we learned it meant "meadow of the calves" in Irish. We offered some grazing pasture to our neighbors, the O'Regan family, and the name has been justified by calves at Clonlea ever since. Besides cows in our fields, there have been many things to get used to, like the well going dry, and cooking with bottled gas from a cylinder that sometimes runs out at a crucial moment if I've failed to check it. And driving eighteen miles to the large supermarket, or seventy miles to the largest supermarket, or even the five miles back to our village market if I've forgotten something. But we can buy meat that hasn't had horrible things added to it, and free-range chicken, duck and turkey. Being by the sea, the fish is always fresh, and the mussels even fresher because we gather them ourselves from an estuary behind the house. And the lamb really tastes like lamb.

Our local friends are an eclectic lot: Irish, of course, but also many Continentals, Scandinavians, a few Americans now, and one Japanese. Although I usually prefer to confine dinners to six or eight, we have had quite a few large parties, and for one

Stone table by the

fishpond

ambitious undertaking a few years ago, we invited 100 people for dinner and dancing in a tent in our lower field. I enjoyed doing all the cooking myself without any help and, I must say, I certainly learned a lot in the process.

It isn't at all like Beverly Hills! When I was growing up there after I lost my mother when I was twelve, my grandmother arranged flowers, the housekeeper had her own ideas about setting the table, and the cook didn't welcome anyone into her kitchen unless it was for a chat or to have a cup of tea. A few years ago, I enrolled in the only cooking course I have ever done, in Bangkok, Thailand, but well before that I had to start learning somewhere. I'm glad most of it has been in Ireland.

(Above right) Ava's garden. In the
distance is the bay where mussels are
gathered.

The Garden

"Isn't This a Lovely Day . . . to be caught in the rain?"

When we first came to live in Ireland (in 1975), there was very little in the way of vegetable and "exotic" ingredients available in the market, so we immediately planted a vegetable garden with things we couldn't buy, like squash, romaine, herbs, spinach, beets and artichokes. We also wanted the

more easily obtained staples: potatoes, carrots, turnips and, of course, cabbages. Much more is available in the shops now, and I can find most of the vegetables I want before the garden is producing, but I always eagerly wait for our own first pickings.

Way beyond our depth in the beginning, we started out with assistance and canny advice from our farmer neighbor, Timmy O'Regan. Although they are our nearest neighbors, the O'Regan farm is out of shouting distance and a five to ten minute walk if you cut across the fields, or a couple of miles by way of the boreens (small lanes). Tim put in our first crop of potatoes and nudged me along through cabbages, carrots, onions, parsnips and beans. I'll never forget one day we were working together, a couple of weeks after planting seeds, and a few things were starting to come up – he scratched gently at a row that had not yet sprouted, looked at me and said, "Ah, I met a bean."

Timmy's term for someone not knowing how to do something is that they are "dull" about it, and I'm sure his help and refusal to accept any payment came from neighborly concern about our dullness in the garden. Timmy has a large farm and family; we couldn't presume on his kindness for very long, so when we told him we felt we should employ someone, he sent along another neighbor: huge, strong, contrary George who, because he couldn't get along with either the Catholic priest or the Anglican minister, became a Seventh Day Adventist, insisted on working Sundays and had lots of ideas, all of which opposed our own – foremost being that the vegetable garden be moved to the other end of the field, nearly an acre away from the convenience of the house. We won that one. Fortunately, George decided to move to another village closer to his church, so we could put out feelers for a professional and were blessed with the arrival of talented, brilliantly witty, irascible Kevin who laid the bones of the lovely garden we have today.

Under Kevin's guidance our garden, like Topsy, just grew, and what was once only meadow land has evolved into many small and different places hidden from each other by trees and shrubbery where – weather permitting – I like to serve lunches.

In Kevin's case we allowed for artistic temperament when, to provide shelter for the vegetables, he obstinately planted pines and other trees from tiny saplings rather than the already established ones we suggested, but they've finally matured into a sturdy grove which we call the forest.

After several years Kevin had greatly extended and enhanced the flowering grounds, adding two fishponds along the way, and when they no longer needed the space, he turned a sheltered patch we shared with the O'Regans for early potatoes into an apple orchard, where a natural spring also ends in a small waterfall Kevin dubbed Niagara. In creating a second vegetable garden and a flower studded hillside, he also had created far too much work for himself, so with his approval we employed Bob to lighten his load.

One of Bob's first noticeable contributions was mowing. He mowed places that had never been mown before and created a tidiness where there had just been wild rough grass. He worked very hard and they got on well for a while, but we started hearing unfounded complaints from Kevin and began to suspect he was becoming jealous. We tried having them work on different days but Kevin was determined that Bob was doing all sorts of terrible things to his garden (which, of course, Bob wasn't) and finally, after being with us for ten years, he quit. Since then we've reclaimed and fenced off from the cows a portion of the upper pasture behind the house, which is kept well cut and where we often close our day with a light supper while watching seabirds circle the bay. He also built us a splendid cage with netting to keep the birds away from our blueberries and which our cat, Larry, considers to be his personal hammock.

Thank goodness for Bob. For several years he took on the huge task alone, but when his daughter, Eileen, and son-in-law, Steve, moved to a neighboring village, we hired Steve to work with Bob and now he and Eileen also look after the house and cats if we are away.

Larry in his hammock

Steve and Eileen are both creative gardeners and when Bob decided to retire we asked Eileen to join our crew. Steve does wonderful things with stones from the beach, and by clearing hillsides to reveal bare rock they have created the best rose garden we've ever had. They also built us a most beautiful rockery as a present for our twenty-fifth anniversary. Others were added, and what was once only gravel in the front yard has become easily maintainable alpines and heather rockeries, along with hydrangeas and wild valerian, and poppies of various types and sizes have blown from other areas or been carried by birds and reseeded into a magnificent display each summer. A great spot for afternoon tea.

8

Much of our life centers in the back garden, a rambling hodgepodge of flowers where Richard plants most of the annuals. We enjoy it all summer if good climate holds, and on the long days we are often able to stay out until twilight fades around eleven o'clock. Sweet peas grow in abundance along a stone wall dividing our vegetable gardens, and one summer, when there was a real explosion of the flowers, I picked an enormous basketful and the only container large enough to hold them was an aluminum tub I usually use for gathering potatoes. As a centerpiece, the mass dwarfed our rather small dining-room table, and because it also seemed a shame for us to be the only ones to benefit, I invited three friends to an alfresco lunch. We shouldn't be inside on such a beautiful day, and since the effect of the substantial sweet pea arrangement would be diminished by the profusion of other flowers in the garden, we set up a larger table in the forest where the trees formed a dense green background.

Much of our life centers in the back garden, a rambling hodgepodge of flowers . . .

I am happiest working with the vegetables, and although the men do the heavy digging and preparing of plots for me, I love being out there thinning new plants, weeding, watering and slug-baiting. Steve and Eileen are wizard weeders, and I would gladly leave it all to them, but among those weeds are edible things – like dill, arugula, parsley, coriander and claytonia – that I am convinced only I can recognize. All of these invariably reseed themselves and spring up each year (especially the dill, which is probably why it is called dill weed), but I never quite trust that they will return, and always plant more, just in case.

I will always be grateful to Timmy for his early tutelage on the basic Irish staples, which we continue to grow, and he always comes down to check our potatoes and spray them for blight if necessary. We are convinced that Irish potatoes really do have a special flavor. I used to think it was because we dug them ourselves, but Richard says that although he still fondly remembers the good potatoes his mother grew, they didn't compare with ours. Maybe it is the Irish soil. We now grow varieties other than the local ones, including the small, narrow potatoes the French call "Rattes," and the exotic blue ones of which Timmy is most suspicious (although I just learned from the doctor that fifty years ago the brother of one of the village bar owners brought some back from Peru and for a while grew them locally). They all seem to be better here than those we have had elsewhere, and I tend to cook them simply so we can enjoy the flavor.

We also now raise more varieties of the other vegetables, including white, golden and pink beets, broad beans, flageolet beans, filet beans, runner beans, sugar snap peas, summer and winter squashes, chard, shallots, onions and many kinds of lettuce. (One of my favorite things is to take a bowl into the garden and make up a salad from as many different lettuce leaves and herbs as possible.)

When I was growing up in Beverly Hills, I never dreamed I would end up in the west of Ireland worrying about cabbage moths that turn into voracious caterpillars, potato blight, the horrid New Zealand flatworm whose only diet is good beneficial earthworms, or the ground being warm enough to plant the broad beans. But then Daddy did have the problem of deer eating my grandmother's roses, and he liked to grow radishes near the swimming pool.

Kevin made us a great table of stones near his fishponds, sheltered by wild fuschia bushes. Where he found the large flat rock he used for the top, or how he even managed to lift it onto the base, he would never reveal, but it is big enough for two or three people to sit around, and if we have more, I put on one of my larger wooden rounds Bob made. I have several tops in different sizes which I use to enlarge the dining table or various tables placed outside for lunch or dinner — on the terrace, in the apple orchard, in the "forest," and next to the upper field where we enjoy the company of cows.

Lunch in the forest

We moved here on Midsummer Day (though just why it is called that when it is actually the FIRST day of summer remains a mystery), and we have celebrated it as an anniversary ever since. That significant day was gloriously clear and sunny, and we have never had a gloomy twenty-first of June since. Because the weather has always been kind to us then, and it stays light so long, we made it a tradition to have a quiet, late lunch – just the two of us, somewhere in the garden – which we stretch to last throughout the rest of the lazy afternoon. We usually end up having wine or champagne out on the end of our land directly above the sea, where so many years ago we toasted the beginning of a lifestyle for which we were highly unqualified. As we did on that day, we always have smoked salmon and brown bread, and since things are beginning to happen in the garden and the greenhouse by that time, I usually make us a salad that includes as much as possible of what is beginning to sprout.

In the company of cows

June 21, 1997, was a beautiful day as usual, but too windy to eat outside. We soon overcame our disappointment, however, because an unusually warm spring enabled me to plant things very early, and for the first time we enjoyed our own zucchini, beets, carrots and a few tiny sugar snap peas on that special day.

A few of our Midsummer Day salads:

Mixed Garden Salad

a mixture of red and green lettuce torn in small pieces

a handful of watercress leaves

cooked sprouting broccoli

cooked, cubed potato

sliced radishes

blanched asparagus fronds

green onions

mushrooms

anchovy, garlic and yogurt dressing

Anchovy, Garlic and Yogurt Dressing

1$\frac{1}{2}$ teaspoons anchovy paste

2 large garlic cloves pureed with a very little bit of salt

1 teaspoon red wine vinegar

a few drops of balsamic vinegar

$\frac{1}{4}$ cup olive oil

plain yogurt

In a mini-processor, blend together the anchovy paste, garlic, vinegars and oil.
Whisk in a few spoonfuls of yogurt.

Chopped Salad

$\frac{1}{2}$ head of crisp lettuce, chopped

$\frac{1}{2}$ cup chopped watercress

2 cooked chicken breasts, chopped

4 oz. smoked ham, chopped

4 tomatoes, seeded and chopped

2 carrots, cooked and chopped

4 green onions, chopped

Shallot Vinaigrette with mayonnaise and blue cheese

Toss all the ingredients with Shallot Vinaigrette to which has been added a spoonful
of mayonnaise and a couple of spoonfuls of crumbled blue cheese.

Shallot Vinaigrette

6 shallots, peeled and cut in pieces

1 tablespoon Dijon mustard

1 tablespoon salt

$\frac{1}{2}$ cup red wine vinegar

a splash of balsamic vinegar

2 cups vegetable oil (or light olive oil) or a mix of both

In a processor, chop the shallots, add the mustard, salt and vinegars,
and then, with the machine running, slowly pour in oil.

Lentil and Vegetable Salad

$^1/_2$ head crisp lettuce, torn in pieces

1 cup lentils, cooked with some cumin and

fennel seeds

cooked sprouting broccoli

lightly cooked zucchini, roughly cut up

cooked carrots, roughly cut up

red and green cabbage, shredded and cut

into $^3/_4$-inch pieces

fennel bulb, cut in small pieces

a handful of cooked pasta shells

toasted pecan pieces

Walnut Oil Vinaigrette

Toss all ingredients, except nuts, with the Vinaigrette and sprinkle the pecans
on top. (Some ground cumin can be added to the salad while tossing.)
*The fennel got there by mistake – I thought it was cumin – but we liked the
combination enough to keep on using it and added fresh fennel as well.*

Tea among the poppies

Walnut Oil Vinaigrette

$^1/_2$ **cup walnut oil**
1–2 tablespoons vinegar or lemon juice
$^1/_4$ **tablespoon salt**
$^1/_2$ **tablespoon Dijon mustard**

Combine all ingredients.

It is a good thing that we have always loved cabbage since we are in the middle of cabbage country. I grow early, late, Chinese and red varieties, as well as other related things such as sprouting broccoli, cauliflower, kale, kohlrabi and, once, purple Brussels sprouts – but they turned green when they were cooked and I decided that, since they are a cold weather crop, I'd rather not freeze my fingers picking them and just buy the very nice ordinary ones in the market instead.

If we win the battle against the offspring of the white cabbage moth (caterpillars) we have lovely and varied crops. (A tip I learned from a book of old garden lore, which seems to deter the moths from laying their eggs, is to surround the plants with grass cuttings.) If we don't achieve complete victory, we still end up with quite a lot of cabbage and its cousins, which I often just shred and stir-fry with simple seasonings, or, in the case of round green cabbage, cook in wedges with a little chicken broth and lots of chopped or dried dill.

14   Some other ways I like to use cabbage are:

Hungarian Cabbage

1 onion, thinly sliced

2 garlic cloves, chopped

vegetable oil

1 white or green cabbage, shredded

chicken stock

1 cup sour cream mixed with 1 teaspoon Hungarian paprika

In a heavy casserole, sauté the onion and garlic in a little oil until just softened, add the cabbage and stir around for a minute or two. Add a bit of chicken stock, lower the heat, cover and cook until the cabbage is just wilted. Stir in the sour cream mixture and bake the casserole at 350° for 20 minutes. Serves 4–6.

I sometimes add crumbled bacon or chopped ham.

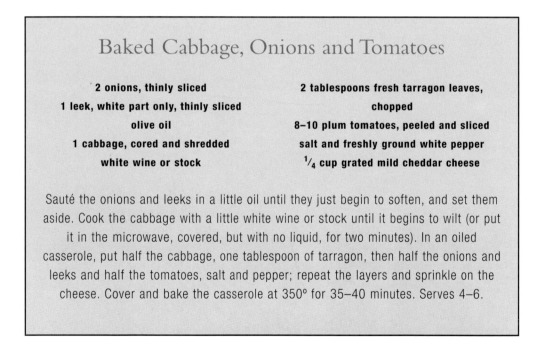

Baked Cabbage, Onions and Tomatoes

2 onions, thinly sliced	**2 tablespoons fresh tarragon leaves,**
1 leek, white part only, thinly sliced	**chopped**
olive oil	**8–10 plum tomatoes, peeled and sliced**
1 cabbage, cored and shredded	**salt and freshly ground white pepper**
white wine or stock	**$^{1}/_{4}$ cup grated mild cheddar cheese**

Sauté the onions and leeks in a little oil until they just begin to soften, and set them aside. Cook the cabbage with a little white wine or stock until it begins to wilt (or put it in the microwave, covered, but with no liquid, for two minutes). In an oiled casserole, put half the cabbage, one tablespoon of tarragon, then half the onions and leeks and half the tomatoes, salt and pepper; repeat the layers and sprinkle on the cheese. Cover and bake the casserole at 350° for 35–40 minutes. Serves 4–6.

Red Cabbage and Bacon Casserole

6 slices of thick cut bacon,

cut in $\frac{1}{2}$-inch pieces

1 large onion, sliced

1 red cabbage, cored and shredded

2 tart apples, peeled, cored and sliced

2 large potatoes, sliced

2 teaspoons caraway seeds

1 tablespoon brown sugar

2 tablespoons lemon juice

1 tablespoon red wine vinegar

1–1$\frac{1}{4}$ cups chicken stock

salt and freshly ground pepper

In a heavy casserole, cook the bacon until as much fat as possible is rendered (without burning the bacon), pour off most of the fat, and then sauté the onion until it is translucent. Add all the remaining ingredients with enough of the stock to just cover, bring it to a boil, cover and bake at 325º for about one hour. Serves 4–6.

I often use kielbasa sausage instead of the bacon, in which case I sauté the onion in a little oil and add the sausage along with the rest of the ingredients.

Chicken with Cabbage

8 pieces of skinless chicken

2 onions, sliced

vegetable oil

1 small cabbage, shredded

2 tablespoons dried dill

salt and freshly ground white pepper

$\frac{1}{4}$ cup dry vermouth

$\frac{1}{4}$ cup chicken broth

In a very hot nonstick saucepan, brown the chicken pieces just a bit, season them with a little salt and pepper, and put them in an ovenproof casserole. Sauté the onions in a little oil for a few minutes to just soften them; toss with the cabbage, dill, a little salt and pepper, and put the mixture on top of the chicken. Pour on the broth and vermouth, and bake the casserole at 350º for one hour.

I use both bone-in and boneless breasts and thighs. Sometimes I make a sauce from the juices brought to a boil, thickened with potato flour mixed with a little water, and some more dill. I also sometimes use cumin instead of dill.

Sorrel
(above) and
gorse
(below)

Foraging for Wild

"Nice Work If You Can Get It – and you can get it if you try"

Things

We don't have to wander very far from our own front gate to find many of the land's wild offerings. At first I only went off in search of wildflowers, but as I began to learn about the edible bounty, the expeditions became much more interesting. I still gather wildflowers even though we have such an extensive garden, because there are masses of violets, primroses, foxglove, yellow iris, Queen Anne's lace (known as "cow parsley") and buttercups that don't grow in the garden. As well as being pretty in vases, the violets and primroses can be sugared and used to decorate cakes and other desserts. I also gather red clover to use in salads, gorse that I infuse with lemon tea to make into sorbet, and wild garlic and sorrel for soups, salads and sauces. Nettles are everywhere, and if you pick the young shoots early enough (wearing gloves – they aren't called stinging nettles for nothing!) they make a nice soup. An estuary behind us has a perpetual mussel bed, some cockles, a few clams and the occasional oyster. Periwinkles and limpets cling to the rocks, while just a little way down the road is a small bay where we net shrimp. Periwinkles (locally called "wrinkles") don't have much taste, but I think they are fun to eat. After boiling them for a few minutes, you can take a pin and pry out the corkscrew-shaped meat. I read that raw limpets are edible, so I tried them (I'll try anything) and rather like them, though I don't know anyone else who does. I once tried substituting them in a conch fritter recipe I brought back from the Caribbean. They were dreadful; it doesn't seem there is any way to cook them so that they don't taste like rubber bands. Also prolific in our waters is pollock, a white fish once aptly described to me by an English friend as resembling "cotton wool with pins in." The cats love it, so I always accept if offered any.

Sometimes in late summer the mackerel run into our little bay and the locals can often pull in as many at a time as there are hooks. It's all very fast and furious fun, and though we don't participate ourselves, we always benefit through the generosity of neighbors. I hurry the catch up to the house because mackerel has a lovely flavor if cooked immediately.

Wild garlic

Sugared Violets and Primroses

freshly picked violet and primrose blossoms

an egg white beaten with a few drops of rosewater

granulated sugar

Make sure that the blossoms are dry and then, with a soft brush, paint the petals with the egg white mixture. Dip each flower in the sugar and leave them to dry for several hours. The primroses should be used as soon as possible, but the violets will keep for a few days.

One violet that somehow got onto Richard's black cap, on a table in the conservatory, stayed there for a couple of weeks before I found it. When I picked it up, it crumbled in lovely violet-colored sugar crystals. AHA! I thought, I'll just make up a batch of violet sugar by drying the flowers longer. Wrong. I think they must have needed to be in the sun room on that black hat, because the sugar just fell off the petals and stayed white. Richard has donated his black cap to the violet sugar cause.

Wild Garlic, Sorrel or Nettle Soup

3 shallots, chopped

2 teaspoons vegetable oil

5 cups wild garlic flowers (or sorrel leaves or nettles)

5 cups good chicken stock

$1/_4$ cup cream

salt and freshly ground white pepper

a little light whipped cream

Sauté the shallots in the oil until just softened, and then add the garlic flowers. Pour in the stock and simmer for about 40 minutes. Puree in a blender (or put through a food mill) and stir in the $1/_4$ cup cream, salt (if necessary) and a bit of pepper. Serve either hot or cold with some whipped cream swirled on top.

At
Home
In
Ireland

20

Wild Garlic or Sorrel Sauce

2 shallots, chopped

2 teaspoons butter

4 cups wild garlic flowers

or sorrel leaves

$^1/_2$ cup good chicken stock

salt and freshly ground white pepper

lemon juice (for the sorrel only)

cream

Sauté the shallots in the butter until just softened and then add the wild garlic or sorrel and the stock. Simmer over very low heat for 30–40 minutes, and puree until very smooth in a blender or food mill. Add salt and pepper (and lemon juice for sorrel) to taste and enough cream to make the sauce a nice consistency. Makes about 1 cup.

I use these sauces mostly on fish, but also on lamb, chicken and some vegetables.
The sauces and soups can be frozen before the cream is added.

Mackerel Paté

$^1/_2$ lb. cooked or smoked mackerel, flaked

$^1/_2$ cup mayonnaise

$^1/_4$ cup onion, finely chopped

1 tablespoon lemon juice

a good pinch of freshly ground white pepper

Puree everything together in a processor, and serve with toast. Serves 6–8.

We have to wait until early autumn for blackberries and field mushrooms, but ever since we have been using mushroom compost on the garden, mushrooms have been turning up all over the place from spring through midsummer. Since we didn't specifically plant them, I consider them wild as well.

Also along our lane in the autumn we pick sloe berries for sloe gin, which neither of us likes, but it seems an amusing thing to make and have on hand. We can easily travel a few miles to wooded areas and gather rowan berries to make a smoky-flavored jelly, and, if we are lucky, chanterelle and boletus mushrooms.

One foraging expedition, however, nearly became a misadventure. Our Swedish friend, artist and former restaurant owner/chef Birgitta Saflund, has generously shared the secret of some of her chanterelle spots with me, and we had gone to search some woods that are more than twenty miles away from home. Birgitta can spot a chanterelle at fifty paces. We found quite a few in a fairly short time, so we decided to move on to an overgrown area to gather heather for centerpieces for Richard's upcoming birthday party, and then to the tops of some boulders to pick rowan berries from the mountain ash trees. Laden with mushrooms, heather and branches of berries, we were nearly at the car when I reached in my pocket for the keys and discovered they were not there. We had just roamed at least two acres of woods and wilderness and the keys could have fallen anywhere along the way. The car was a temporary rental from a firm in Cork City two hours away and we had

**Mushrooms in
the potato patch**

no second set or a second car. We also were about three miles from a telephone. There was nothing else to do but go back. After tramping around with a sinking heart, I must have been guided by benevolent leprechauns to look into a crevasse in a boulder under a mountain ash tree. Eureka!! By another stroke of luck, that morning I had attached a plastic ornament filled with sparkle dust to the otherwise unobtrusive key chain; without it, I doubt that even the leprechauns could have helped me.

When I asked Birgitta for some Swedish chanterelle recipes, she said they weren't particularly different from other mushroom recipes, but because chanterelles have a much better flavor, the Swedes use them extravagantly when they are in season. She gave me a few suggestions: "Pick mushrooms, don't lose car keys. Clean them, wipe lightly, cut large ones into rough pieces. Sauté gently (small piece butter) until all water has evaporated. They can then be used with great variety."

At
Home
In
Ireland

Chanterelle Salad

a good mixture of lettuce leaves　　　**bacon, cooked and finely chopped**

chanterelles, sautéed in butter　　　**good vinaigrette**

"Or add cream to sautéed chanterelles, reduce cream in approximately half volume. They are fantastic added to an omelette."

"Or make a soufflé."

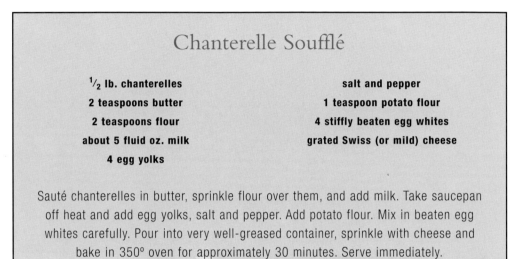

Chanterelle Soufflé

$1/2$ **lb. chanterelles**　　　　　**salt and pepper**

2 teaspoons butter　　　　　**1 teaspoon potato flour**

2 teaspoons flour　　　　　**4 stiffly beaten egg whites**

about 5 fluid oz. milk　　　　**grated Swiss (or mild) cheese**

4 egg yolks

Sauté chanterelles in butter, sprinkle flour over them, and add milk. Take saucepan off heat and add egg yolks, salt and pepper. Add potato flour. Mix in beaten egg whites carefully. Pour into very well-greased container, sprinkle with cheese and bake in 350° oven for approximately 30 minutes. Serve immediately.

Birgitta also gave me a recipe for rowan jelly, which is a good accompaniment to game, and I've included the one we use for sloe gin.

Rowan Jelly

3 lbs. rowan berries

$1^{1}/_{2}$ lbs. apples

sugar and water

Stem the berries. Roughly chop the apples, leaving on the skin, and put them in a pan with just enough water to cover and simmer for about an hour. Drip through a jelly bag overnight. Measure the juice and add 1 cup of sugar for each cup of juice.
Pour the juice and sugar into a heavy pan, bring to the boil stirring to dissolve the sugar and boil hard until the setting point is reached.

Sloe Gin

1 lb. sloes	**1 bottle (a fifth) of gin**
$\frac{1}{4}$ cup sugar	**a few drops of almond essence**

Prick each sloe a few times with a large needle and put them all in a jar. Dissolve the sugar in the gin and pour it over the sloes. Add the almond essence, cover the jar and put it in a dark place for about three months, shaking it occasionally. When it is ready, strain the gin into another bottle.

We Californians have been taught to be wary of mussels. In fact, even though he was brought up in a coastal town which depended largely on its fishing industry, neither Richard nor I had tasted any until we moved here. We soon discovered that we have the great bonus of a mussel bed behind the house (with a field or two in between), and it has become our favorite way of entertaining visitors. First we make sure the tide is low, put on boots, and then make our way through the nettles down to the shore. Next, I instruct everyone to follow my footsteps so as not to get stuck in the mud – however, I have been known to get it wrong and fall in the mire myself – and then we start picking the mussels off the rocks. Usually, at first, novices can't see any at all, but once their eyes become attuned and they realize that there are MILLIONS, there is no stopping them. We end up bringing back many more than we need . . . but there is a bonus to that, too, because we get the guests to clean them and I freeze the extras for Richard and me to have later when we are alone. Actually we all pitch in on the scrubbing process because it does take a lot of effort, and it is important to remove the "beards." Still, guests really seem to enjoy it, and, when they are finally allowed to sample the results of their efforts, always comment that they are the best mussels they've ever eaten. No doubt the mussels are fresher than any they've ever had before.

Put the scrubbed mussels in heavy pots over high heat. It is not necessary to add water. Because they are so fresh, they will supply plenty of liquid (liquor) to steam themselves open (discard any that do not open). I then take them out of their shells, pull off any remaining beards, rinse them to remove grit, and, most of the time, serve them on the half shell, just with garlic butter and fresh bread. I keep a supply of washed shells on hand, so all I have to do is fill shallow baking dishes with the clean shells, put a mussel and a bit of melted or softened garlic butter on each, and stick them under the broiler until they are hot. If we have found any cockles, I cook them along with the mussels. It is, after all, the country of Molly Malone.

Garlic Butter

8 garlic cloves
2 shallots
4 oz. each unsalted and lightly salted butter, softened
2 tablespoons chopped parsley

In a processor, chop together the garlic and shallots, add the butter and parsley and process a little longer. Makes enough for about 50 mussels.
I sometimes add a bit of ground cumin to the garlic butter and often now substitute olive oil for the butter.

I have found that if plain, steamed mussels are frozen for longer than a month or so, they lose the fresh taste and are best chopped, but if they have been frozen for only a short while, I can hardly tell the difference. I also freeze any extra garlic butter as well as the (well strained) "liquor."

A few more things we do with mussels:

Pasta with Mussels

Gathering mussels with Portia Nelson

6 garlic cloves, chopped
4 shallots, chopped
3 tablespoons fruity olive oil
$2^{1}/_{2}$ cups cooked mussels, whole or chopped
$^{1}/_{4}$ cup mussel liquor
16 oz. linguine or fettucini
1–2 cups basil leaves, chopped

Sauté the garlic and shallots in the olive oil until fragrant but not brown, then add the mussels and liquor and set aside until the pasta is cooked. Put the mussel mixture in a heavy pot, bring just to a boil, add the drained pasta, and toss over low heat with the chopped basil. Serves 4.

Mussel and Fresh Tomato Soup

6 dozen mussels, steamed and in their liquor

6 garlic cloves, chopped

3 shallots, chopped

olive oil

8 tomatoes, peeled, seeded and chopped

white wine or vermouth

hot pepper sauce

chopped parsley

Strain the mussel liquor through fine muslin and set it aside. Remove any beards from the mussels and set them aside. Sauté the garlic and shallots in a little olive oil until just softened. Add the tomatoes, stir them around for a minute or so, and then pour in the mussel liquor and enough wine or vermouth to cut the saltiness. Add a few drops of hot pepper sauce, and bring the liquid just to a boil. Put in the mussels, heat them through, and divide them and the liquid between large soup bowls. Sprinkle the soup with chopped parsley. Serves 4.

If I have any of the soup left, I freeze it to use as a sauce thickened with more tomatoes.

Mussels in Guinness came about by chance. We were given an enormous amount of farmed mussels, which are really just as good as those we gather ourselves, and very useful if the weather is bad or we don't want to do all the work required when dealing with wild ones. They need no cleaning, just de-bearding, but they sometimes do not render as much liquor. Such was the case when our houseguest, Mélisande, found that a bottle of Guinness she had opened earlier had gone flat. I hate to waste good things, so we added the flat brew to the pot and ended up with a different and nicely flavored broth.

Mussels in Guinness

6 dozen mussels, steamed and in their liquor

1 onion, chopped

olive oil

1 bottle of Guinness

Strain the mussel liquor through fine muslin, and sauté the onion in a little olive oil until just softened. Pour in the liquor and a cup of Guinness, and bring the broth to a boil — taste and add more Guinness if necessary, and then add the mussels and heat through. Serves 4.

Our own compost, along with seaweed and some farmyard fertilizer, at one time provided enough nourishment for the garden, but as it expanded we added a commercial mushroom compost. The bounty from that is enormous – around 100 pounds each spring/summer season. We've been told that some purveyors treat their compost with a chemical to arrest growth – but ours clearly hasn't learned that trick yet. The compost certainly pays for itself, which is great, except that there is no way I can use that many mushrooms. And it will happen all over again (though not quite to the same degree) in the autumn, when the wild field crop emerges. I'm not complaining! It is always exciting – like an Easter egg hunt. I have found quite a few ways of dealing with the harvests, including giving bags full to all our friends, especially the doctor, who is mad for them, the postman, the fish man, the painter, the plumber and, once, the man who came to re-enamel our bathtub.

Some of the mushrooms are huge (I have stuffed a large chicken with just one, chopped up), most are mid-sized and lots are small buttons. I freeze quantities of them chopped and lightly sautéed, made into duxelles, purees and soup, and try to use them all before the next explosion comes along!

Not Classic Duxelles

4 shallots, finely chopped   **1 lb. mushrooms, finely chopped**
1 tablespoon butter and 1 tablespoon oil   **1 tablespoon lemon juice**

Sauté the shallots in the butter and oil for a few minutes, add the mushrooms and lemon juice and continue cooking, stirring over low heat until all liquid disappears.
Makes about 1$\frac{1}{2}$ cups. Freeze in small portions.

Mushroom Soup

2 shallots, chopped   **1$\frac{1}{2}$ lbs. mushrooms, roughly chopped**
5 cups chicken stock   **2 tablespoons cream**

Soften the shallots in a little of the stock and then stir in the mushrooms and the remaining stock. Simmer for 40 minutes, cool, and whirl in a processor until fairly smooth – there should be visible bits of mushroom. Add cream before serving. Serves 4.

For puree, cook the shallots and mushrooms in only a small amount of stock for about 30 minutes, cool and puree until smooth. Freeze the soup **before** adding the cream, and freeze the puree in small portions.

Rowan
berries
and
heather

Chicken Stuffed with Mushrooms

2 shallots or a small onion, chopped	a 3–4 lb. roasting chicken
chicken stock	salt and freshly ground pepper
1 lb. mushrooms, chopped	chicken stock

Soften the shallots or onions in a little stock, and mix with the raw mushrooms. Stuff the mixture into the chicken, salt and pepper the outside, and roast at 350° (for about 20 minutes per pound), basting occasionally with chicken stock. Serves 4.

Mushroom and Nut Paté

$\frac{1}{2}$ lb. shallots, chopped	1 cup each pistachios, almonds and
$\frac{1}{2}$ tablespoon vegetable oil	hazelnuts, finely chopped
$\frac{1}{2}$ lb. mushrooms, chopped	salt and freshly ground white pepper
grated rind and juice of 1 orange	

Sauté the shallots in the oil until just softened, add the mushrooms and continue to cook over low heat, stirring, for about five minutes. If mushrooms render much liquid, cook longer to reduce. Stir in the rind, juice, nuts and some salt and pepper. Spread the mixture into a baking dish and bake, covered, at 350° for about 45 minutes. Cool, and then puree in a processor. To serve, mix in some chopped olives or chopped kumquats or Greek yogurt or . . . Makes about 2 cups.

Mushroom and Liver Paté

5 or 6 large shallots, chopped

vegetable oil

2$^1/_2$ cups mushrooms

2 hard-boiled eggs

$^2/_3$ cup chicken livers

juice of 1 lemon

salt, freshly ground pepper and cayenne

1–2 tablespoons cream cheese, softened

Sauté the shallots in a little oil for a few minutes. Combine the mushrooms, eggs, and shallots in a processor; add the livers and lemon juice and process a little longer. Spread the mixture into a baking dish and bake, covered, at 350º for 30 minutes. Cool, process the mixture until smooth, taste and add salt, pepper and cayenne. Stir cream cheese into paté before serving. Makes about 1$^1/_2$ cups.

Both of the patés freeze well (before adding the chopped fruits, nuts, yogurt or cream cheese).

Mushroom and Barley Casserole

4 shallots, chopped

2 garlic cloves, chopped

1 tablespoon vegetable oil or butter

1 lb. mushrooms, roughly chopped

1$^1/_2$ cups chicken stock

1 cup pearl barley

1 teaspoon dried marjoram

chopped parsley

Sauté the shallots and garlic in the oil or butter until just softened, stir in the mushrooms, and cook a few minutes longer. Put the mushroom mixture in a baking dish, pour in the chicken stock, stir in the barley and marjoram, and bake, covered, at 325º for about 40 minutes or until the liquid is absorbed. Sprinkle with chopped parsley. Serves 4.

Mushroom and White Beet Salad

1 1/2 cups cooked and peeled white beets
1 small cucumber, peeled, salted and drained
1 apple, cored and peeled
salt and freshly ground white pepper
1/2 lb. firm, closed cap mushrooms, roughly chopped
3 tablespoons chopped green onions, white part only
Shallot Vinaigrette, mayonnaise and plain yogurt

Chop the beets, cucumber and apple into half-inch cubes, adding salt if necessary (the cucumbers will be somewhat salty), and pepper. Then add the mushrooms and onions, and toss with a dressing made of Shallot Vinaigrette mixed with a little mayonnaise and plain yogurt. Serve on its own or on top of mixed greens that have been tossed with a light lemony vinaigrette. Serves 4–6.
The salad is just as good using red beets, but you get a pink salad instead of a white one.

Chard and Mushroom Roulade

1 lb. mushrooms, roughly chopped
vegetable oil
3/4 lb. cooked chard leaves, squeezed dry and roughly chopped
salt and freshly ground pepper

4 medium eggs, separated, whites beaten to soft peaks
a little hot pepper sauce
12 oz. light cream cheese, softened and mixed with 1/4 cup chopped chives

Sauté the mushrooms in a little oil until softened and liquid has cooked away. In a processor, finely chop the chard and mushrooms with some salt and pepper, and then add the egg yolks and hot pepper sauce until well combined. Fold in the beaten egg whites and spread the mixture into a jelly roll tin (10 1/2 x 15 1/2 x 1 inch) lined with lightly oiled parchment. Bake at 400° for 25 minutes. Cool.
While it is still in the tin, cut the roulade in half crosswise, spread the cream cheese and chives on each piece, and roll them up. Chill and cut into half-inch pieces.
Makes 20–24 pieces.
I often freeze the roulade, in its tin, for a week or so.
From time to time, I'm not sure why, the roulade won't roll. When this happens
I cut it into squares and make "sandwiches."

Mixed garden pickles

(Facing) clockwise from top left: Golden cauliflower, fennel, yellow and chioggia beets, zucchini, potatoes, carrots and artichokes

Harvest Rewards

"You say tomato, I say tomahto"

Each autumn when we start looking at the seed catalogues, and the following spring when we start the planting, we always forget that if we are lucky and things grow well, we will end up having too much. We then happily give extras to friends without gardens of their own, occasionally to strangers who stop to ask directions, and most of all to our friends who are restaurateurs. They all know that we often have a surplus and it really pleases me when Philippe or Sabine, who own Blairs Cove restaurant, call to ask if I have lettuce, dill or coriander (cilantro), or if I can give them some claytonia, which is wonderful for garnishing.

The freezer also gets its share of the extras, mainly in the form of purees for soups, but I think it is more rewarding to deal with the excess by making pickles, relishes and chutneys.

Here are a few favorites:

Coriander Chutney

4 Granny Smith or medium cooking apples

2 medium onions

2 garlic cloves

2 medium zucchini

1 red pepper

$1^3/_4$ cups red wine vinegar

1 teaspoon dry coriander seed, crushed

$^1/_4$ cup green coriander seed, crushed

a piece of bruised ginger

3 allspice berries and a few peppercorns,
tied up in muslin

$1^1/_4$ cups brown sugar, loosely packed

$^1/_2$ cup chopped cilantro (fresh coriander)

$^1/_2$ cup chopped mint

Peel and chop the apples, onions, and garlic. Chop the zucchini. Seed, core, and chop the pepper, and simmer them all in a heavy saucepan with the vinegar for about 30 minutes. Add all remaining ingredients except the chopped cilantro and mint, and simmer for about an hour, until thick. Remove the tied up muslin and ginger before sealing the chutney in sterilized jars. Makes a little more than 2 pints. Stir in fresh chopped coriander and mint whenever serving.

Pickled Shallots

Stringing shallots

4–6 lbs. small shallots

brine of 2 cups kosher salt dissolved in 4 quarts water

2 pints white vinegar

2 tablespoons sugar

2 tablespoons pickling spice,
including a few dried chilis

peeled garlic cloves

dill heads or dill seeds

Soak the unpeeled shallots overnight in half of the brine. Rinse them, drop them in boiling water for one minute, and then peel them and soak them again in the rest of the brine for 24–36 hours. Rinse well. Bring the vinegar, sugar and pickling spice to a boil and then cool. Put a clove of garlic, a chili and a dill head (or the seeds) in sterilized preserving jars, fill with shallots, and cover with the vinegar.

Mustard Piccalilli

3 lbs. zucchini

3 lbs. onions, carrots and cucumbers combined

1½ cups kosher or pickling salt

7 cups white vinegar

6 dried chilies

6 whole cloves

a 1-inch piece of ginger, bruised

1 cup sugar

6 tablespoons dry mustard

3 tablespoons turmeric

Chop all the vegetables, mix them with the salt, and leave for 24 hours. Drain and rinse very well. Simmer 5 cups of the vinegar with the chilies, cloves, and ginger (all tied in a cheesecloth bag) for 20 minutes. Add sugar, and when it has dissolved add the chopped vegetables. Simmer 15 minutes. Mix mustard and turmeric with remaining vinegar, stir in, and simmer 5 minutes more. Put into hot sterilized jars and seal. Makes about 6 pints.

Curried Piccalilli

4 lbs. green zucchini

3 onions

3 red peppers, seeded and cored

3 cups light brown sugar

3 cups white or cider vinegar (or both)

4 tablespoons medium curry powder

2 teaspoons pickling spice tied in a muslin bag

In a processor chop the zucchini, onions, and peppers. Dissolve the sugar in the vinegar, add the curry powder, pickling spice, and vegetables, and simmer for about five minutes. Spoon into hot sterilized jars and seal. Makes about 6 pints.

We always use one of these pickle relishes mixed into both tuna salad and ham salad.

I read that because it contains so much nitrogen, hair is a great nutrient for beans and peas, so when I go to Breda, our hairdresser, in the spring, I bring the trimmings home to bury in the beds where we will be planting those particular vegetables. At first, Breda was startled at my request, but now she has come to expect it, and when she knows I'm coming in, saves that day's clippings for me as well. My husband declared he wanted no part of "any hair-raising schemes," but since it comes from a book of country wisdom, I expect Timmy O'Regan would heartily approve. At any rate, I'm convinced that the multitudes of healthy beans and peas we now get are completely due to the hair around their roots.

Beet Relish

1¹/₂ lbs. raw beets
1¹/₂ cups white vinegar
1¹/₂ cups sugar
2 medium onions, chopped
2 lbs. cabbage, chopped
2 tablespoons caraway seed
¹/₄ cup grated horseradish root

Cover whole beets with cold water, bring to a boil, and simmer for 15 minutes. Peel them and chop finely. Bring the vinegar and sugar to a boil, add beets, caraway seed, and the rest of the chopped vegetables, and simmer for 10 minutes. At the end stir in the horseradish. Put into hot, sterilized jars and seal. Makes 4–5 pints.

Dill-Pickled Green Beans

2¹/₂ cups white distilled vinegar
2¹/₂ cups water
4 tablespoons kosher salt
8 garlic cloves, peeled
pickling spice
8 heads of dill
2 lbs. slim, straight green beans, trimmed
4 sterilized pint jars

Bring the vinegar, water, and salt to a boil and stir to dissolve the salt. In each of the jars put two garlic cloves, a pinch of pickling spice, a dill head, the beans, and another dill head on top. Pour in the vinegar mixture and seal the jars.
Let stand a few weeks before using.
This can also be done with asparagus. Although we have an asparagus bed, it is precious stuff and I can't spare any, so I buy some to make the pickles.

All these pickles and relishes can be processed in a boiling water bath for 20 minutes, but because they contain large amounts of vinegar, I've been assured by professionals that it is not really necessary and alters the texture.

Our friend Peggy made pickled cabbage for a large event and gave us some to taste. We liked it and I asked for the recipe, which she was glad to give me, but she didn't know how to do it for less than 300 people! I broke it down as best I could, and I think I got it right.

Pickled Cabbage

1 cup sugar

1 cup white vinegar

$1\frac{1}{4}$ cups water

1 teaspoon mustard seed

1 teaspoon celery seed

1 teaspoon salt

2 green cabbages, chopped

5 red peppers, cored and chopped

$1\frac{1}{2}$ lbs. carrots, peeled and chopped

Combine the sugar, vinegar, water, mustard seed, celery seed and salt, and stir until the sugar has dissolved. Add the chopped vegetables, stir around a bit, and put in a clean jar. Store in the fridge. Makes considerably less than 300 servings!

Also in the area of yielding too much is our little apple orchard. We often retreat there on warm summer days and used to amuse ourselves by counting the burgeoning apples; but now that the trees are really producing, I spend more time trying to think of how to use the crop. As always, thank goodness for the freezer and for friends to whom we can give some, and from whom we welcome suggestions. Maureen O'Hara says just to core them, put them unpeeled and roughly chopped in a heavy pan with a little water, heat until mushy, and then freeze them in usable portions.

I have a handy gadget that peels, cores and slices apples all at once, so I freeze lots of them that way (without cooking the slices). I also like to freeze peeled, uncooked cubes to use in salads.

Garden platter: chioggia beets and carrots, white beets and zucchini

Some apple things:

Apple and Fennel Soup

1 leek, chopped

1 onion, chopped

1 cup white wine

12 tart apples, peeled, cored and chopped

1 tablespoon chopped fresh apple mint (or mint)

1 teaspoon chopped fresh marjoram (or a little less dried)

5 fennel bulbs, chopped

4 pints chicken stock

cream and chopped mint

Simmer the leek and onion in a little of the white wine until softened, add the apple and herbs, simmer a bit longer, and then add the fennel, chicken stock and the rest of the wine. Simmer for about 40 minutes and puree in a blender or food mill until very smooth. Whisk in some cream before serving either hot or cold. Garnish with some lightly whipped cream and chopped mint. Serves 10–12. The soup can be frozen before adding the cream.

Layered Apple "Cake"

$\frac{1}{4}$ cup sugar

$\frac{1}{4}$ cup water

1 tablespoon lemon juice

8 large apples (not cooking), peeled and sliced

4 oz. butter

26 wheatmeal biscuits (or 30 graham crackers), crushed

$1\frac{1}{2}$ teaspoons cinnamon

$\frac{1}{2}$ cup chopped, lightly toasted almonds

brown sugar

Dissolve $\frac{1}{4}$ cup of sugar in the water, add lemon juice, and then simmer the apples in the syrup for about 10 minutes. Melt the butter, mix in the crushed biscuits and cinnamon and stir until lightly toasted. In an 8–10 cup baking dish, put half the crumbs, cover with half the apples and then half the almonds. Repeat the layers and sprinkle a little brown sugar on top. Bake at 375°, uncovered, about 25 minutes. Since this is not really a cake, serve it from the dish, warm or cold. Serves 8–10.

Apple and Rhubarb Chutney

3 medium tart apples, peeled, cored and chopped

2 lbs. trimmed rhubarb, cut in 1-inch pieces

2 large onions, chopped

$1^1/_2$ cups golden raisins

$1^1/_4$ cups brown sugar, loosely packed

2 cups cider vinegar

$1^1/_4$ teaspoons medium curry powder

1 teaspoon chopped fresh ginger

$^1/_2$ teaspoon (scant) ground cloves

$^1/_2$ teaspoon cinnamon

a few drops of hot pepper sauce

Put all the ingredients in a heavy saucepan and bring them slowly to a boil. Reduce the heat and simmer, stirring often (leave uncovered) for about two hours. Spoon into hot, sterilized jars. Makes about 4 pints.

Apple Butter

4 lbs. apples

2 cups apple cider

juice and rind of 1 lemon

Cut apples into quarters, core but do not peel, and remove bruised bits. Put them in a heavy pan with the cider, bring to a boil and cook, stirring, until the apples are soft. Sieve, or put through a food mill, and then measure the pulp, return it to the pan, and add the lemon juice and rind. For each cup of pulp add:

$^1/_4$ cup brown sugar

$^1/_2$ teaspoon ground cinnamon

$^1/_8$ teaspoon ground cloves

$^1/_8$ teaspoon pumpkin pie spice or allspice

$^1/_8$ teaspoon ground ginger

Cook over low heat, stirring frequently until thickened — about two hours. To test, put a bit in a plate. It is done if no liquid forms around the edge (or when you draw a spoon across the pot it leaves a trail). Makes about 6 cups.

In the garden, it is just the opposite in the spring, after everything has been planted but is not yet up. Then there is hardly anything but the watercress growing in our small stream, and soon some radishes. When Richard sometimes jokingly complains that all he has had to eat is radish stems, it isn't much of an exaggeration. We love radishes, especially a variety called Pink Beauty that stays crisp even when it is almost the size of a golf ball. They are particularly nice steamed, and don't lose their pink color. I also chop the stems and leaves (specially for Richard!) and use them as cooked greens and in soups. Something else that comes early is asparagus. We don't cut the first spears but let them grow and use the young fronds. They are delicious and make a very attractive garnish.

The watercress is always welcome and continues growing for many months. It spreads and gets so overgrown that we have to pull it out, but it comes back so quickly that I always have some and use it a lot for soup, dips, salads and on pasta.

Pasta with Watercress

2 or 3 garlic cloves, chopped
2 tablespoons best olive oil
16 oz. fettucini, cooked and drained
$3/4$ cup yogurt
6 cups chopped watercress
salt and pepper
asparagus fronds, blanched

In a large heavy saucepan, heat the garlic in olive oil until just softened, add the (still hot) fettucini, and over low heat stir in the yogurt and watercress. Keep tossing it all until it is well warmed but not so hot that yogurt will curdle. Add a little salt and lots of freshly ground pepper. Top with asparagus fronds. Serves 4.

Cream, or combined yogurt and cream, can be substituted, but we are quite happy with the plain yogurt — and it is so much healthier.

Radishes with Blue Cheese

1 lb. radishes

3 tablespoons mayonnaise

2 heaped tablespoons crumbled blue cheese

Chop radishes and steam for two minutes. Drain very thoroughly. In a heavy saucepan over low heat, stir together the mayonnaise and blue cheese, add the chopped radishes and continue cooking until just heated through. Serves 6–8.

Cutting watercress in
the garden

Watercress Soup

1 shallot, chopped

oil

7 cups chicken broth

7 cups chopped watercress

Cook the shallot in a little oil and broth for a few minutes. Add the watercress and cook over low heat until wilted, then add the rest of the broth and simmer for about 30 minutes. Serves 6.

Puree this in a blender. Cream or plain yogurt may be added. Serve either hot or cold. The soup can be frozen before adding cream or yogurt.

A Castle & Other

Aunt Dellie at Lismore
Castle (facing)

Irish Things

"Look to the Rainbow"

When I was twelve, my father took me on my first trip to Ireland to visit my Aunt Adele at Lismore Castle, which became her home when she retired from the stage to become Lady Charles Cavendish. Although Aunt Dellie was widowed after ten years, she continued to live in the castle with my grandmother for company, until she remarried, and even then she returned nearly every summer. Sometimes I visited her without Daddy, and she invited Richard and me to Lismore the first summer we were married. It made for a wonderful extended honeymoon and, although he is part Irish, gave Richard his initial taste of the country. A few years later, after we had moved to Ireland ourselves and exchanged life in a castle for life in a cottage, we tried to visit my aunt as often as possible during the times she was there by herself.

Most of the staff returned to their homes in nearby Lismore village at night, and, my aunt having been widowed a second time, we knew she felt better if there were a few of us rattling around that huge place. Occasionally I would ask Aunt Dellie if we might include some of our own friends. Angela Lansbury and her husband, Peter Shaw, who lived not far away sometimes came to lunch along with Hurd Hatfield, and twice we shared the time with our very dear friends Betty White and Allen Ludden.

Except for Daddy, guest visits were limited to no more than four days, which we thought was a sensible arrangement even though it often meant our having to leave for just a few days before coming back again. At one of those times, when we had obediently departed for the allotted period, upon our return my aunt said that she wished we hadn't gone and that the real reason for her strict dictum was that she knew only about four days' worth of menus.

Delia, her cook, told me she would have welcomed more challenge than repeating the same menus, but even though they became predictable, during those four days we knew we could count on wonderful lunches and dinners. Both my aunt and my father liked very simple food, and Delia had a way of making even the basic things special. I am grateful that I was able to coax quite a few recipes (or "receipts" as they often say here) from her.

Here are some of the Lismore menus and Delia's "receipts."

Two luncheon menus:

SMOKED SALMON • IRISH STEW* • MIXED GREEN SALAD • BREAD AND BUTTER PUDDING WITH BLACK CHERRIES*

This was Aunt Dellie's favorite menu for visiting Americans. The stew is made with chops rather than stew meat, and everyone loved the bread and butter pudding made slightly more sophisticated by the addition of black cherries.

STUFFED TOMATOES • WHITE DEVIL* • MIXED GREEN SALAD • GOOSEBERRY FOOL* WITH SPONGE CAKE

We always had salad and a cheese board at lunchtime, but never cheese at dinner – Aunt Dellie said the cheese at night made you dream. Dinner started with soup, included vegetables from the garden, a simple main course and usually ended with nursery-type puddings.

*denotes recipe is included

"Fools" are like creamy fruit soups – the sponge cake is for sopping up.

Two dinner menus:

FRESH PEA SOUP* • POACHED WHOLE SALMON (PEAL) • NEW POTATOES • BROAD BEANS • SUMMER PUDDING*

This was also a favorite menu. Peal are salmon weighing under ten pounds, and these were caught in the Blackwater River just below the castle.

FRESH TOMATO SOUP • ROAST CHICKEN WITH BACON • BREAD SAUCE* • NEW POTATOES • BABY BEETS AND THEIR GREENS • JUNKET AND FRESH BERRIES

The new potatoes were tiny – sometimes the size of a grape. My grandmother always said that when potatoes were new and small they had no starch.

Bread sauce is used as an accompaniment to roast chicken. It was Allen Ludden's favorite thing along with summer pudding, which was always made when the wild blackberries were ripe.

Aunt Dellie loved junket, and had it on the menu more often than anything else. The berries were only added when she had guests other than family.

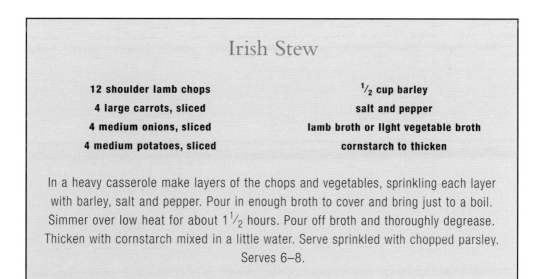

Irish Stew

12 shoulder lamb chops	1/2 cup barley
4 large carrots, sliced	salt and pepper
4 medium onions, sliced	lamb broth or light vegetable broth
4 medium potatoes, sliced	cornstarch to thicken

In a heavy casserole make layers of the chops and vegetables, sprinkling each layer with barley, salt and pepper. Pour in enough broth to cover and bring just to a boil. Simmer over low heat for about 1 1/2 hours. Pour off broth and thoroughly degrease. Thicken with cornstarch mixed in a little water. Serve sprinkled with chopped parsley.
Serves 6–8.

Bread and Butter Pudding with Black Cherries

1 16-oz. can pitted dark cherries in juice

3–4 slices good white bread, lightly buttered

cinnamon

5 whole eggs and 2 yolks

1 cup sugar

3$\frac{1}{2}$ cups milk, scalded

1 teaspoon vanilla

water

Drain the cherries and put them in a 10 x 6 x 2–inch baking dish. Put the bread slices on top and sprinkle with cinnamon. Beat the eggs and yolks, beat in the sugar, and, still beating, add the milk and vanilla. Pour the mixture through a sieve over bread. Put the baking dish in a roasting pan and add enough water to come halfway up the sides of the dish. Bake at 350° for 50 minutes.

White Devil

chicken stock

2 large whole chicken breasts

1 cup heavy cream

1 teaspoon English mustard

1 tablespoon Worcestershire sauce

1 tablespoon mushroom ketchup

spinach

Bring the chicken stock to a boil, put in breasts, and simmer for 8–10 minutes until just firm. Cool in the stock, and take the meat off the bones in strips. Lay the strips in an ovenproof serving dish. Whip cream a little, mix in other wet ingredients, and pour over chicken. Bake at 350° for 15 minutes, then put under a hot broiler for a few minutes to lightly brown. Serve on a bed of lightly cooked, roughly chopped spinach. Serves 6.

Mushroom ketchup comes in bottles a little bigger than Worcestershire sauce. I have seen it in the United States in shops specializing in food from the British Isles.

Gooseberry Fool

1 lb. gooseberries, topped and tailed

1 tablespoon butter

$^1/_3$ cup sugar

1 egg yolk

2 tablespoons sugar

$^2/_3$ cup milk

$^2/_3$ cup heavy cream, whipped

Gently cook the gooseberries with the butter in a covered pan until soft. Stir in the $^1/_3$ cup sugar until melted, and puree the fruit. Blend the egg yolk with the 2 tablespoons sugar in top of a double boiler. Bring the milk just to the simmer and pour into the egg mixture, stirring. Cook, stirring constantly, over boiling water until thickened. Leave to cool, stirring occasionally to prevent a skin forming. When the custard is cool, stir in the gooseberries, and then fold in the cream. Chill and serve with fingers of sponge cake.

Aunt Dellie liked this served on plates rather than bowls, and it really was much easier to sop it up with the cake than using a spoon.

Fresh Pea Soup

2 teaspoons butter

1 onion, chopped

sprig of mint

$1^1/_2$ lbs. peas and their pods

about 2 pints chicken stock

a bay leaf

heavy cream and sugar to taste

whipped cream

chopped parsley

Melt butter and add chopped onion and mint. Cook for a few minutes but do not brown onions. Add peas and pods, breaking up pods. Add stock and bay leaf, cover, and simmer for an hour. Remove pods and bay leaf and puree rest of soup. Add cream and sugar to taste. When serving, top with a spoonful of whipped cream and sprinkle on some chopped parsley. Serves 6.

Summer Pudding

1 loaf of white bread, slightly stale

butter

2 lbs. mixed berries: blackberries, red currants, raspberries, etc.

$^3/_4$ –1 cup sugar, depending on sweetness of berries

Trim crusts from the bread, and cut it into pieces that will neatly fit the inside of a six-cup mixing bowl (pudding basin). Butter the inside of the bowl and line it with the bread (you won't need all of the bread). Cook the berries and sugar over gentle heat until the berries are soft. Spoon the berries and some of their juice onto the bread and cover with a layer of bread cut to fit (save any extra juice). Put a plate that fits inside the bowl on top of the bread, and on this put a two- or three-pound weight. Chill overnight. Unmold. Juice should have thoroughly soaked the bread; if not, spoon on reserved juice where needed.

I often make summer pudding. Our friend Dick De Neut liked it so much that he made one for a dinner party right after he returned from visiting us. Perhaps he did it wrong. The consensus of opinion was that he had made a berry sandwich.

Bread Sauce

$1^1/_4$ cups milk

a small onion stuck with 6 cloves

1 teaspoon salt

1 bay leaf

1 allspice berry

a few grinds of pepper

1 oz. butter

2–2$^1/_2$ cups white bread crumbs

Simmer the milk with the onion and seasonings for 30 minutes over very low heat. Remove onion, bay leaf and allspice berry. Add butter and stir in bread crumbs until sauce is thick with no free milk visible.

Aunt Dellie's closest Irish friends were two wonderful old ladies, Clodagh Anson and the marvelous writer Molly Keane. Molly's dark humor and insight were apparent in her novels, but Clodagh – perhaps the funniest woman we've ever known – was totally unaware of it and never seemed to realize why we all screamed with laughter when they were invited to lunch at Lismore. The ladies seldom came for dinner because Molly lived a fair bit away, and

though her house was in view of the castle, Clodagh still had to drive – and both women were lethal behind the wheel.

When Aunt Dellie felt she could no longer make the trip to Lismore, and until we lost them, we continued to see her old friends whenever we could. Molly was revising one of her plays with a character based on my aunt when she died at age ninety-two, and Clodagh ended her days in a convent where she gave drinks and bridge parties in her room. Both of them visited us. One of my favorite memories is of Clodagh wielding her net (with the same enthusiasm with which she maneuvered a steering wheel), with her skirt hitched up under her belt as she went shrimping with our sons, Kevin and Tyler. Another was a luncheon at her house when she had a couple of local girls in to help and the less experienced one stopped short of Richard, who was the last to be served. It amused him enough not to say anything the first round, but, when the girl turned away as he waited expectantly for the next dish, he quietly mentioned it to Clodagh, who diplomatically remarked that she didn't think Mr. McKenzie had taken quite enough of the egg mousse. Seeing Richard's clean plate and realizing what she had done, the embarrassed girl said, "Polly put me off!" I'm not sure just how Polly put her off but it has become a catch phrase whenever I make a blunder – which is often.

Clodagh's Egg Mousse

4 teaspoons gelatin dissolved in 1$\frac{1}{4}$ cups hot consommé

1 tablespoon Worcestershire sauce

3 tablespoons sherry

2$\frac{1}{2}$ cups heavy cream, whipped to soft peaks

12 hard-boiled eggs, chopped

salt and freshly ground white pepper

parsley sprigs to garnish

Mix the Worcestershire sauce and sherry into the consommé mixture and let cool to lukewarm. Fold in the whipped cream, eggs, pepper and salt (if necessary), turn the mixture into a soufflé dish and refrigerate until set. Garnish with parsley sprigs. Serves 8.

Although she had help, Molly Keane was a very good cook herself, and always knew exactly what was going on in the kitchen. Here are a couple of simple traditional recipes she gave me:

Dublin Cally

2 lbs. potatoes, peeled and quartered

salt

4 green onions with green stalks, chopped

$\frac{1}{2}$ cup milk

$\frac{1}{4}$ cup melted butter

Boil the potatoes until they are soft, drain, and let them dry. Mash them with a little salt. Simmer the onions in the milk for about 15 minutes, until they are soft, and mix into the potatoes. Be sure not to make the mixture too wet. To serve, make a well in the potatoes and pour in the melted butter. Serves 6–8.

Another name for this potato dish, "champ," is apparently Northern Irish, and in West Cork our neighbors grew up calling it "brusie." Our favorite version, "colcannon," has cooked cabbage or kale mixed into the potatoes.

Kedgeree

2 oz. butter

$\frac{1}{4}$ cup cream

2 cups flaked smoked haddock

8 hard-boiled eggs, chopped

$1\frac{1}{2}$ tablespoons Worcestershire sauce

salt and freshly ground pepper

4 cups warm, cooked rice

chopped parsley

Melt the butter and stir in the cream. Mix in the fish, eggs, Worcestershire sauce, and salt and pepper, and heat thoroughly before tossing with the rice. Turn into a warm serving dish and sprinkle on the chopped parsley. Serves 6.

I often make Kedgeree with leftover salmon in place of haddock, and because I almost always have odd bits of smoked salmon in the freezer, I throw that in as well.

After what, sadly, turned out to be our last visit to Molly Keane, we stopped to see Darina Allen, one of Ireland's foremost cooks, whose highly acclaimed Ballymaloe Cookery School has become world renowned. A visit to Darina is always a treat and

With the Irish writer Molly Keane in her library

her vegetable garden is the prettiest I've ever seen. Darina created a lovely crazy quilt design in her garden when she separated vegetable types by bordering many plots with box hedge, cornflowers, herbs and the like. Enhancing an already lovely effect, the garden meanders around the remains of some wonderful stone sheds, with even a lookout point for the children high on the wall which encloses the grounds. We gladly welcome an invitation to lunch after her morning classes, knowing it comes with a guarantee that all produce will be from that wonderful garden. Once, when Richard and I happened to fly out of Cork on the same plane as Darina, she boarded with a basket of her own free-range eggs and fresh-picked tomatoes, which she blithely shoved into the compartment over our heads, which was a bit worrying, but we all arrived unsquashed and unsplattered.

Discussing lamb
with Justin
McCarthy

We don't eat a lot of meat, but when I do want some – particularly lamb – I make an effort to go to Justin McCarthy's excellent butcher shop in the town of Bantry. Not only is Justin fourth generation in his family business, he was also once mayor of Bantry. Dressed in white aprons and jaunty white derby hats, he and his staff (mostly his sons) have great flair and sell only the highest-quality meats. Justin offers the old-fashioned kind of personal assistance seldom encountered in other parts of the world these days. In the finest sense of the word, he is a true gentleman.

Whenever Richard and I sample a selection of Irish cheeses and like one in particular, it invariably turns out to be Gubbeen, which is made by our good friends Giana and Tom Ferguson. Giana says that when she and Tom come across their cheese in a foreign place, they are always surprised and just a little uncomfortable, because it is rather like finding their children somewhere they shouldn't be.

The Fergusons had been making cheese for the family for quite some time before they decided, in 1979, to try producing it commercially for just a few shops. Nine years and many prestigious awards later they began exporting, and now they market fifty tons a year – which means all the milk from 100 cows is being made into cheese every day and Giana's initial little enterprise has become bigger business than they had ever anticipated. Since their farm is closer than the village, I usually purchase cheese directly from Giana, but Richard says the real reason is to visit their lovely sow, Olivia. No doubt true, because Tom often lets me hold one of her babies.

Everyone in the United States seems to think that corned beef and cabbage is the most traditional of all Irish dishes. In truth, it really is not found much around the country and certainly everyone does not cook it on St. Patrick's Day – in fact, unlike in America, no one does much on St. Patrick's Day except perhaps go to the pub.

Actually, what seems to be the most traditional Irish dish is bacon and cabbage. When we first came here, there seemed to be more bacon available than anything else, and not sure what to do with it, I asked for help from our neighbor Marie. (I have since learned that bacon in Ireland is more or less equivalent to uncooked ham in the U.S.)

Marie, now widowed, lives with her son on a beautiful farm just across the small cove from us. She helped us with the housework for the first few years we lived here and has remained a cherished friend ever since. Marie is no longer able to ride her bicycle to call on us, so I drive up the hill to her brightly painted place for a chat, or bring her down for tea and biscuits in her favorite spot among our apple trees. I have been treated to a lot of country wisdom during those talks and I will never forget the day, when I was visiting in her kitchen, she took a cake from the oven, put her ear close to the top of it and pronounced it done. She said that she had always "listened" to her cakes, and now so do I. (If you hear it hissing it's not done.) Marie told me that, when she was growing up, they used to cure the bacon in a barrel near the open turf fire and that was where the smoky flavor originally came from. Now, when she buys bacon, she gets it from the local butcher because he cures his own and it is closer to the flavor she remembers than the commercially packaged ones. I have taken her cue and buy it from him as well. Here is how Marie told me to do **Bacon and Cabbage:**

Steep the bacon in water overnight and then throw out that water. In a large pot, cover it again with water and bring it to the boil. (She then likes to go through the process again but her sister-in-law thinks that makes the bacon "too fresh.") A 2–3 lb. bacon cooks at a simmer in about $1\frac{1}{2}$ hours. Test by sticking in a thin knife. It should not meet too much resistance as it gets to the center. Use the water to cook quartered pieces of cabbage and kale or turnips as well.

Tea in the

apple orchard

Richard doesn't cook (except spaghetti, potato salad, tuna casserole, and egg sandwiches) but he does sometimes show me recipes he's liked the sound of in magazines, and recently he heard an Irish lady on the radio talking about her grandmother's way of stuffing a chicken with oatmeal. It was so simple that he remembered the recipe: "Oatmeal, onions, seasoning and water," he said. "The lady said it has a nutty flavor, not to use too much water, and stuff the bird loosely because it expands," he added. I tried it with the next chicken, and it was really very good. Then Richard got inventive and suggested trying it with muesli. That was good, too.

This is the way I worked it out:

Oatmeal Stuffing

$^1/_2$ cup chopped onions

about $^1/_4$ cup water

1 cup dry oats (not instant) or muesli (not too sweet)

salt, pepper and 1 teaspoon dried thyme

Cook the onions in a little water to soften, mix them with the oatmeal,
and add more water until the mixture just begins to stick together.
Add seasonings and stuff loosely into a chicken.

One of the most Irish things of all is soda bread. I have been pleased with the
results I get from the following recipes.

Brown Soda Bread

$^3/_4$ cup oatmeal

$1^1/_4$ cups whole wheat flour

$1^1/_8$ cups white flour

1 teaspoon bicarbonate of soda

1 teaspoon salt

$1–1^1/_2$ cups buttermilk

Grind the oatmeal in a processor and then combine it with the flours, soda and salt. Stir in
enough of the buttermilk to form a soft dough. Turn the dough out onto a floured board and
with lightly floured hands form it into a round loaf. Put the loaf on a lightly oiled baking
sheet, flatten it slightly, cut a deep cross in it with a floured knife, and bake at 375° for
about 40 minutes. Test with a knife and knock on the bottom to be sure it sounds hollow.

I also use Marie's hissing test for soda bread. Friends have had good results
using a soda bread mix they took back to the States. It is also now available
in some U.S. specialty markets.

White Soda Bread

4 cups plain white flour
$^1/_2$ teaspoon salt
1 level teaspoon bicarbonate of soda
about 1–1$^1/_2$ cups buttermilk

Mix the flour, salt and soda in a bowl and add enough buttermilk to form a soft and slightly sticky dough. Turn the dough out onto a floured board and with floured hands pat it into a round. Transfer the loaf to a lightly oiled baking sheet, flatten it out a bit, and cut a deep cross into it with a floured knife. Bake at 375° for about 40 minutes. (Test with a knife, and tap bottom to see if it sounds hollow.) Cool on a rack and wrap in a tea towel to keep it soft.

Breakfast by the sitting room window

Clifftop picnic by
the sea

Regatta Sunday
(Facing) In the upper field

Picnics at Home

CHAPTER FIVE

"I'm Putting All My Eggs in One Basket"

' Further Afield

We try to eat outdoors as often as weather permits. Within a few miles' radius, a short walk or, in fact, just a few feet away, are some of the most beautiful picnic settings imaginable.

Weather doesn't always permit, however, and counting on being able to have outdoor parties in the summer also involves prayer and trust in luck. We've had summers of uninterrupted sunshine with drought conditions, and summers of uninterrupted drizzle and fog. Sometimes it seems we can have all the seasons represented in a single afternoon. In spite of this, I often plan picnics, and only a few times I have been challenged by the elements. One memorable Fourth of July while we were laying out picnic cloths on the back lawn in blazing sunshine, the sky turned midnight black like a solar eclipse. It happened so quickly that when lightning crackled, there was a sort of "end of the world" wonderment and the many guests rushed into the conservatory. Fortunately none of the other food had been brought out yet, but I had chicken breasts on the barbecue which could not be taken inside. When torrential rains came, everyone had settled in dry comfort and found it hilarious watching Richard try, unsuccessfully, to shield me with an umbrella while I continued cooking. We were both soaked to the skin. Although the electrical power was knocked out, the party continued by candlelight. The power wasn't restored for three days and people still talk about the eeriness of that sudden and dramatic transformation. Complete with nature's own fireworks, it's certainly an Independence Day I'll never forget!

Sometimes it seems we can have all the seasons represented in a single afternoon.

Unless the meal is in our own garden, I don't use china or glass and, as much as I love the idea of setting up a table and chairs in beautiful remote places, I think the joy of eating out in the open is diminished if it becomes too complicated or burdensome. So I only use lightweight, unbreakable dishes and colorful cloths for picnics away from home, and to that effect I have collected a lot of plastic glasses, plates, platters and bowls. Just about the only thing I can sew without total disaster is the hem on a tablecloth, and over the years I have made quite a few and am always on the lookout for fabric that will go with the yellow, blue, green and red of the dishes.

In case we may be driving far from home and discover an irresistible new place for an unplanned scenic lunch, I always keep a set of picnic necessities in the car. There is usually a small village fairly near where cheese, fruit, soft drinks, wine and cold meats are available. Sometimes we have been really lucky and found fresh bread and even locally smoked salmon, trout or mackerel. Amongst the necessities, I keep dishes, cups, a tablecloth, paper napkins, plastic cutlery, a tube of mustard, a sharp knife and, of course, a corkscrew. Although there is plenty of very good wine in Ireland, it is not necessarily obtainable in just one store, and not always near home, therefore the corkscrew at hand is a must. I might happen upon a new wine at a good

**Morning coffee at
"The Point"**

price and want to taste it before buying more than one bottle, and at those testing times, I fervently hope that no one we know will see me, all alone, in the car surreptitiously pouring myself a cup of wine. So far, so good. I think.

On the seaside of our land is a promontory we call "The Point." We can easily carry picnic paraphernalia to it and often go out there for coffee, tea, drinks, lunch or – sometimes on the long days – even dinner. The thick and bouncy grass makes eating alfresco quite comfortable and, with the ocean on three sides, the setting is beautiful, peaceful and so beguiling that Richard and I were standing on this spot when we finalized our decision to live in Ireland. It is also where, after I lost my father, I spent a good deal of quiet, healing time. It is a very special place. One clear, sunny morning when I saw that the hay had been freshly cut in our upper field, I remembered reading something about roasting lamb in hay and rushed off to Bantry to buy a leg of lamb from Justin and give it a try. I came home with great anticipation as well as a superb leg of lamb. There was lots of hay aside from what was already in bales, and a few of the bales made a great table. Sorrel also grows at the edge of the field. We have always loved sorrel soup, which is good hot or cold, so several hours later we had a picnic of:

COOL SORREL SOUP • LEG OF LAMB IN A NEST OF HAY AND HERBS* • SALAD FROM THE GARDEN • FRUIT AND CHEESE

Leg of Lamb in a Nest of Hay and Herbs

several large fistfuls of hay
small bunches of rosemary, thyme, mint and oregano
4 crushed garlic cloves
a 4–5 lb. leg of spring lamb
salt and pepper
water

Gathering the
hay with Henry

Lay half the hay and herbs and all the garlic in a large, heavy casserole. Salt and pepper the lamb, put it on the hay, top with the remaining herbs and hay, and add about a tablespoon of water. Cover the casserole and bake at 350° for about $1\frac{1}{2}$ hours (or to an internal temperature of 145°–150°) until medium pinkish.

The hay can be freshly cut or beginning to dry – either way it has a wonderful aroma when you open the lid. (If hay is very dry, sprinkle on a tablespoon or two of water before cooking.)

Since it was a picnic that first special day, we had cold lamb, but I often do this for dinners for visitors from the city, letting them smell the aroma when it comes out of the oven. Most people are astonished at the use of hay, and that it doesn't catch fire.

Dividend: I have chard and beets in the garden all summer long, and I usually combine them with leftover lamb to make a sort of crustless pie.

Lamb and Chard (or Lamb and Beet) Pie

1 cup chopped onion

2 garlic cloves, chopped

olive oil

2 cups chopped cooked lamb

2 cups cooked and chopped chard leaves or beet greens

1 cup cooked and chopped chard ribs, (or cooked, chopped beets)

2 eggs, beaten

2 tablespoons cream

2 tablespoons mayonnaise

at least 2 tablespoons chopped rosemary

1 teaspoon nutmeg (freshly ground if possible)

salt and freshly ground pepper

Sauté the onion and garlic in a little olive oil until just softened and combine them with the remaining ingredients. Put the mixture into a deep 9-inch pie dish and bake at 350° for about 40 minutes. Serve cool. Serves 4.

Over the years I have managed to match many of my bowls, plates and baking dishes to baskets of corresponding size (a few I have had specially made) and always use them for large picnics in the garden. I rely on them and plan much of the food around what container will fit which basket, and it never occurred to me that our decision to paint the kitchen would have repercussions affecting my basket collection.

When we saw the setting, the fact that this 200-year-old farmhouse had been somewhat eccentrically restored didn't matter, but we knew some alterations were in order. Adjoining a large dining room, the previous owners had built a very small kitchen, without cupboards, and an even smaller larder to store the

provisions. Beyond that was a long, high ceilinged room which held horse tackle, the pump and assorted odd bits. I coped with the cramped space far longer than good sense decrees before the pump in the large back room was given its own little house in the garden, and the saddles and such were removed to the barn where they should have been in the first place. We then lowered the ceiling and installed wooden cabinets, paneled the plaster walls to combat damp, called in Dublin Tony – house painter extraordinaire – to finish it off, and I gained a new, warm and comforting kitchen. The former one became a fine pantry where I hang all my baskets from the low-beamed ceiling.

**Seventh of July
picnic in the
garden**

Years ago I was visiting a friend at Fox Studios (in Los Angeles), who had used baskets to decorate a movie kitchen set. I was about to tell him how effective I thought they were when the director objected to them. He said, "Real people don't hang baskets in their kitchens." I've done exactly that ever since. This time, however, in taking down the baskets in order to paint the ceiling, Tony found that they were all infested with woodworm, and had to be treated or burned to prevent the plague from spreading.

Quite a few people were expected for a Fourth of July (actually seventh of July) picnic and barbecue while our friends from Washington, the Beards

(Judge Larry and Doctor Lillian), were to be with us. I knew the kitchen would be finished just in time for me to get a few things done before they arrived, and that I would be able to do more each morning while they slept off their jet lag. But I certainly hadn't anticipated that I might have a basket crisis with many of my old reliables being condemned. Luckily, a few only needed their handles cut off – but the ones I use without liners to hold deviled eggs (the eggs don't slide around), chips and crudités couldn't be in contact with food due to the woodworm treatment, and some of the specially made ones got the death sentence. I unearthed every ceramic and glass container in the house, finally managed to find almost enough corresponding baskets, and ended up buying only a couple of new ones that we will try to keep free of the nasty little pests.

After a not very good start to a summer of mostly fog and misty rain, the day of the picnic was the best one we'd had since the previous year, and because the invitations read "it will NOT rain," everyone decided that I had a direct line to the patron saint of good weather. Whatever, I was very grateful. Three infants in their carry-cots slept in the safe comfort of the greenhouse while the many other children ran around the garden, up and down the hills, and hid among the trees. We barbecued marinated chicken breasts and turkey frankfurters. Having rounded up enough baskets to hold everything else on the menu, I was relieved to be able to serve the food as originally planned, and we ended the party late in the evening with the police sergeant singing "Danny Boy," "Old Man River" and "Lili Marlene."

LAYERED MEXICAN DIP* • ROASTED NEW POTATOES WITH YOGURT CHIVE DIP • CHARD AND MUSHROOM ROULADE* • SMOKED SALMON PATE WITH HOMEMADE CRACKERS* • SMOKY DEVILED EGGS*

* * *

BARBECUED TURKEY FRANKFURTERS • BARBECUED MARINATED CHICKEN BREASTS* • PICKLED LOIN OF PORK* • MARINATED CABBAGE* • MIXED BEAN SALAD • PASTA, TOMATO AND ZUCCHINI SALAD* • CARROT AND HORSERADISH SALAD • CURRIED RICE AND CORIANDER SALAD • CAESAR SALAD

* * *

RHUBARB CRUMBLE CAKE* • BROWNIES • PEANUT BUTTER AND OATMEAL COOKIES

The **Mexican Dip** is just layers of refried beans, sour cream mixed with taco seasoning, chopped avocado, olives, tomatoes, onions, shredded lettuce and cheese. It is always a favorite with our Irish and Continental friends who have come to expect it, so it is now always included on any outdoor party menu. I usually use Greek yogurt instead of sour cream because it is thicker than the sour cream produced in Ireland, and I like it better. The refried beans can be hard to find, but pureed kidney beans work quite well, and it really is the taco seasoning (which is easy to find in Ireland) that is most important. Carrot and Horseradish Salad is the old standard shredded carrot and raisin salad (I use golden raisins) with horseradish added to the mayonnaise. I make the Curried Rice and Coriander Salad with cooked white rice, curry powder (of course), mango chutney, and lots of chopped cilantro (fresh coriander).

Just before the picnic I saw a package of what was labeled "Real American Style Frankfurters." Thank goodness we tried a couple before using them for the party because they were terrible, and the turkey ones we've been buying for years remain a much better choice.

Unless noted, the following recipes were sufficient quantities as part of a picnic for forty people.

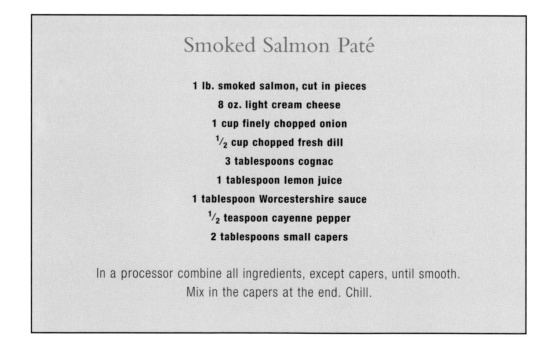

Smoked Salmon Paté

1 lb. smoked salmon, cut in pieces

8 oz. light cream cheese

1 cup finely chopped onion

$^1/_2$ cup chopped fresh dill

3 tablespoons cognac

1 tablespoon lemon juice

1 tablespoon Worcestershire sauce

$^1/_2$ teaspoon cayenne pepper

2 tablespoons small capers

In a processor combine all ingredients, except capers, until smooth.
Mix in the capers at the end. Chill.

Whole Wheat Crackers

2 cups whole wheat flour
1 scant teaspoon salt
$^1/_2$ cup plus 2 tablespoons water
5 tablespoons oil
sesame seeds
whole wheat flour

Mix all ingredients in a processor until dough forms a ball on the blade – if this doesn't happen add up to 2 tablespoons more water. Divide the dough into four pieces and flatten into rectangular shapes. Knead each piece through thickest setting on a manual pasta machine. To do this, after putting the dough through the first time, fold it twice, pat it back into a rectangle and roll through. Repeat the process two or three times and then roll the dough through the next setting. Lay the fairly long piece of dough on a lightly floured board, cut it in half, sprinkle on a good amount of sesame seeds, and roll the dough pieces through until they reach the best thickness (on my machine this is number four). Lay the strips on nonstick or oiled baking sheets. Run a pastry wheel lightly along ragged edges and across strips to make squares or rectangles. Bake at 425º for 8–10 minutes until crisp. Cool, and break the crackers apart, also breaking off edges. There will be at least 100–120 crackers.

Smoky Deviled Eggs

2 tablespoons liquid smoke
$^1/_2$ cup light soy sauce
1 cup white vinegar
2 cups water
1 tablespoon brown sugar
12 hard-boiled eggs, peeled
mayonnaise

Boil together liquids and sugar, cool slightly, and while still warm pour the marinade over the eggs and refrigerate for at least four days. Cut the eggs in half, mix the yolks with enough mayonnaise to make a fairly soft consistency, and then, with a pastry bag, pipe the mixture into the cut whites.

Double the recipe for 40 people.

The outside of the whites turns a dark mushroom color – which doesn't sound very attractive, but the cut sides stay white and the yolks stay yellow, so the overall appearance is fine.

Marinade for Chicken Breasts

$^1/_2$ cup fruity olive oil

juice of 2 or 3 lemons

5 garlic cloves, chopped

$^1/_2$ cup dry vermouth

a few drops of lime oil

2 tablespoons fresh rosemary leaves, finely
chopped

salt and pepper

Combine all ingredients in a blender or small processor.
Marinate skinned chicken breasts for at least one hour, but longer is better.

*I order lime oil from an English catalog. It is available from specialty food stores
and catalogs in the U.S.*

Pickled Loin of Pork

4 bay leaves

2 teaspoons dried thyme

2 teaspoons juniper berries, crushed

a few allspice berries, crushed

1 teaspoon dill seed

1 teaspoon white mustard seed, crushed

1 teaspoon white peppercorns, freshly ground

$^3/_4$ cup dark brown sugar

about a quart of 10 percent brine*

2 2-lb. pork loins, boned

2 carrots, roughly chopped

2 onions, cut in half and each stuck with 2 cloves

some celery leaves

Mix the herbs, spices and sugar into the brine and boil until the sugar has dissolved.
Cool. Put the pork in a strong plastic bag, cover with the brine mixture,
then seal the bag so that the pork stays covered. Put the package in a bowl
and refrigerate, turning daily for six days. Tie the pork loins with string to make them
into log shapes, and put them in a heavy pot with the carrots, onions, celery leaves and
enough water to cover. Simmer for about an hour, and leave them in the liquid to cool.
The pork can be frozen in its brine and defrosted and cooked later.
*A 10 percent brine is made by dissolving enough salt (not iodized) in water until an egg
will float – about $1^1/_2$ cups salt to 1 gallon of water.

Marinated Cabbage

3 tablespoons kosher, pickling or sea salt

1 cabbage, shredded

(or equivalent of red and green mixed)

1 thinly sliced red or white onion

$\frac{1}{2}$ cup olive oil

$\frac{1}{2}$ cup lemon juice

juice of 1 orange

1 tablespoon grated fresh ginger

1–2 tablespoons chopped mint

Sprinkle 2 tablespoons salt on cabbage and leave for three hours. Sprinkle 1 tablespoon salt on onions and leave for one hour. Mix both together and soak in ice water for one hour, drain (rinse if too salty) and dress with the olive oil, lemon juice, orange juice and ginger. Toss with mint.

Pasta, Tomato and Zucchini Salad

16 oz. penne pasta, cooked and well drained

5 cups tomatoes, chopped, peeled, and seeded

5 cups cubed and cooked zucchini

2 cups fresh basil leaves, roughly chopped

1 cup fresh tarragon leaves, chopped

2 cups chopped Walla Walla onions (or green onions)

crumbled feta cheese

garlic vinaigrette

Toss all the ingredients together and dress with a vinaigrette that has one or two garlic cloves, pureed, with a little salt whisked into it.

Every year on Regatta Sunday we have a picnic on one of the beaches, ostensibly to watch the yacht and dinghy races, but it is really just an excuse to have a picnic. By some miracle it has never rained on Regatta Sunday either – yet.

The food is set up on whatever rocks we hope will be above the high tide mark, but sometimes we get it wrong. In one way or

another the Neuberger family always try to arrive by sea. Once, when Anthony
Neuberger windsurfed in, we used his board for a serving table but had to
keep moving it up the beach to save our lunch from the approaching tide.

There are usually about twenty to thirty adults and a few children. I do most
of the food, but some of the others bring things as well, and I am particularly
happy if they bring the desserts, because I really don't like sweets and would

**Surfboard serving
table at Regatta**

much rather make the other dishes. Our friend Frankie Ross has been
organizing the picnic with me since her daughter Siobhan, now a teenager,
was a baby, and she makes a point of bringing food that children like. Adults
like it, too, but they have to move pretty fast to get any of Frankie's Sesame
Chicken or Brownies. A few of the others own restaurants, so there are
various offerings from them, and Rabbi Julia Neuberger always provides
hummus and a splendid pasta salad. Everyone brings wine. We certainly
never run short of good things to eat and drink, and though we often have to
flee to higher grounds, our group usually remains until well after the races
are over, when most spectators have gone home or – more likely – to their pub
of choice.

A typical Regatta menu and some recipes – quantities for twenty to twenty-
five people – as part of a picnic buffet:

MEXICAN DIP* • FRESH OYSTERS • CRUDITES WITH HONEY, GARLIC AND ORANGE MAYONNAISE* • ARTICHOKES WITH DILL SAUCE*

* * *

POACHED SALMON WITH CORIANDER SAUCE* • MARINATED ZUCCHINI* • TURKEY AND CABBAGE SALAD* • FRANKIE'S SESAME CHICKEN* • HUMMUS NEUBERGER* • JULIA'S PASTA SALAD • SMOKED POTATO* SALAD • CUMIN BREAD*

* * *

FRANKIE'S BROWNIES • BIRGITTA'S APPLE CAKE • JEANNE'S NECTARINE PIE

When I take the **Mexican Dip** to a picnic away from home, I put only the refried beans, sour cream/taco seasoning, avocado, and olive layers into a rectangular plastic serving dish and add the rest at the picnic spot. Even if they are well drained, the tomatoes continue to yield a lot of juice which makes the whole thing runny and spills out all over the car, rendering husbands cross for the rest of the day.

For the **smoked potatoes** I bake (or microwave) waxy potatoes in their jackets until they are almost done, and then when the barbecue is beginning to die down I spread them around the outer edge, throw on some smoking chips, cover, and let them smoke for 30–45 minutes. For the salad I peel them, cube them, and use a mayonnaise to which I've added a little liquid smoke. Or, if the skins haven't gotten too charred, I crisp them in the oven and we have them with Greek yogurt and chives.

Honey, Garlic and Orange Mayonnaise

2 eggs and 1 yolk
$1/2$ teaspoon dry mustard
3 garlic cloves mashed with $1^1/_4$ teaspoons salt
3 tablespoons orange juice
2 tablespoons orange marmalade
3 tablespoons honey
$2^1/_2$ cups vegetable oil

In a blender or processor mix eggs, mustard, garlic, orange juice, marmalade and honey. With mixer running, pour in oil in a steady stream until mayonnaise thickens.

Artichokes with Dill Sauce

14 3-inch artichokes

3 sprigs of fresh rosemary

3 garlic cloves, crushed

olive oil

$^1/_2$ cup mayonnaise

$^1/_2$ cup yogurt

1 tablespoon dried dill

1 tablespoon chopped fresh dill

Boil artichokes in water with a little olive oil, the garlic, and rosemary for about 45 minutes or until leaves pull easily away. Drain. When the artichokes are cool enough to handle, cut them in half from the bottom, removing chokes, leaving larger leaves attached to hearts. Mix mayonnaise, yogurt and dill and put a spoonful in each artichoke cavity.

Coriander Sauce

2 shallots, chopped

chicken stock

2 cups cilantro (fresh coriander) leaves

salt and pepper

about 1–2 cups mayonnaise and yogurt combined

Soften the shallots in a little chicken stock, add the cilantro and a bit more stock. Simmer until the cilantro is soft, let cool, and then puree. Add some salt and pepper if necessary, and whisk the puree into mayonnaise mixed with yogurt.

Marinated Zucchini

5 yellow zucchini

5 green zucchini

olive oil

white wine vinegar

3 garlic cloves

salt and pepper

$^1/_2$ tablespoon each of chopped fresh oregano and parsley

1 teaspoon fresh thyme

Thinly slice the zucchini, sprinkle with salt, and let drain for about one hour. Rinse and dry, and then sauté in olive oil until just wilted. Sprinkle with vinegar, garlic, salt, pepper and herbs and leave to marinate overnight.

Turkey and Cabbage Salad

For the turkey:

1 cabbage, chopped

1 large onion, chopped

1 tablespoon vegetable oil

1 tablespoon cumin seed and 1 teaspoon ground cumin

a 10-lb. turkey

Toss the cabbage and onion with the oil and cumin and cook, covered, in the microwave on high power 1–2 minutes to wilt, or stir-fry a few minutes. Stuff into the turkey and roast at 350° (about 25 minutes per pound). Cool and refrigerate.

For the salad:

the turkey meat, shredded

1 pint plain yogurt mixed with 2 tablespoons cumin seed

salt and freshly ground white pepper

the cabbage stuffing

1 pint plain yogurt

1 cup green onions, chopped

Toss the shredded turkey with the yogurt/cumin seed mixture and some salt and pepper. Toss the cabbage stuffing with some salt, pepper, cumin and enough of the plain yogurt to just thinly coat it, then place the turkey, cabbage and onions in layers in a serving dish or on a platter.

The yogurt/cumin seed mixture is best made well in advance of using in order to soften the seeds.

Frankie's Sesame Chicken

8 chicken breasts, boned, skinned, and split

2 eggs beaten with $1/4$ cup milk

seasoned flour

1 cup bread crumbs mixed with $1/3$ cup sesame seeds

butter and vegetable oil

Slice each split breast into three or four pieces and pound to flatten a bit. Dip each piece of chicken in egg mixture, then in flour, and last in bread crumbs and sesame seed. Chill for an hour and sauté in oil and butter until golden brown.

Hummus Neuberger

4 cups garbanzo beans (chickpeas), drained
$1/4$ cup water
$1/4$ cup olive oil
3 garlic cloves, chopped
1 teaspoon salt
juice of 3 lemons
1 cup chopped fresh cilantro (coriander)

In a processor mix the beans, water, olive oil, garlic, salt and lemon juice until smooth.
Stir in the cilantro. Best if done a day ahead.

Cumin Bread

3 cups flour
1 tablespoon sugar
2 tablespoons baking powder
1 teaspoon dry mustard
4 teaspoons ground cumin
1 teaspoon cumin seed, crushed
1 teaspoon salt
3 beaten eggs
$1^1/_2$ cups milk
$1/3$ cup oil

Stir together the dry ingredients. Separately, whisk the eggs, milk and oil. Mix together until
smooth(ish). Pour into a well-oiled loaf pan, and bake for one hour at 350° or until the
bread tests done. Cool for 15 minutes in pan and then turn out onto a rack.
Slice the bread and cut the slices in half.

For all-day outings, I try to plan two-stage picnics where we have the first half
in one location and the second in another.

There is a beautiful spot in County Kerry where three lakes are fed by various
streams and waterfalls. I always take visitors there for a picnic beside one of

A waterfall in
County Kerry

the streams. A small road leads to my favorite place, which is relatively untraveled, and we hardly ever see another person, although we are sometimes joined by an inquisitive sheep or cow. We can park the car out of sight but near enough that carrying the food is easy, so we have plenty of time for a leisurely lunch. Later on, I almost always swim before we head towards home and have fruit and cheese or tea in the company of sheep at the top of Healy Pass, overlooking another spectacular lake.

Also in Kerry, on the way to Killarney one day, while walking in the woods with friends we came across a waterfall with plenty of places nearby to lay out a picnic. We hadn't brought lunch that particular time, but as soon as I could, I went back and scouted the area and found another waterfall to use as a second location for two-stage picnics.

Our friends Moira, Deirdre and John told us about a wonderful ruin of a seventeenth-century manor house but warned us that "something" doesn't want people to eat there. They had attempted picnicking there several times before and on each occasion clear, sunny skies had abruptly turned to torrential rain. I wanted to see for myself, so one beautiful day I invited them to join us for another try. As I was photographing the beginning of our picnic, the hex struck, cloudless skies began to blacken, and rain tipped down halfway through the meal. We valiantly carried on for a few minutes but finally had to give up and pack everything away. As soon as we had done this, the rain stopped. Moira surprised us with a bottle of Clicquot, and we ended the day, sipping in blazing sunshine, sitting on the crumbling walls of the courtyard – for me a particularly special final touch because that is the only champagne my father ever kept in the house.

Some of my containers for carrying food are attractive enough to use for serving as well, the handiest of these being a set of bright yellow covered bowls that are stacked in groups of four and held together by a carrying handle. I found them years ago in a supermarket in Limerick and, unfortunately, only bought two sets. I could use more and have never come across them again. I searched a long time to find shallow baskets to hold twelve-inch-round covered bowls, but I was eventually successful, and I have found those bowls really useful for carrying larger salads. We always carry food and utensils in baskets, some of which are hampers that also serve as small tables. For picnics "further afield," sometimes leftovers I have in the fridge inspire me to organize an impromptu excursion, and other times I plan it all ahead.

Salmon Salad Niçoise

8 oz. cooked salmon, flaked

$\frac{1}{2}$ lb. sugar snap peas, blanched

4 medium potatoes, cooked and cubed

olives

capers

romaine and iceberg lettuce

$\frac{1}{2}$ lb. cherry tomatoes, halved or quartered

olive oil vinaigrette

Toss together all salad ingredients except tomatoes and put them in a plastic bag. Put the tomatoes in a separate bag. Carry them to the picnic in a chilled container and mix with the vinaigrette (made with $\frac{1}{2}$ cup olive oil, 1–2 tablespoons vinegar or lemon juice, $\frac{1}{4}$ teaspoon salt, and $\frac{1}{2}$ tablespoon Dijon mustard) just before serving. Serves 4–6.

Here are a few more picnic dishes:

Grilled Chicken and Kumquat Salad

4–6 chicken breasts*, char-grilled or broiled, cut in 1-inch pieces

16 kumquats, seeded and roughly chopped

a bunch of watercress, chopped

6 green onions, white and green parts, chopped

Walnut Lime Vinaigrette

$^1/_4$ cup toasted walnuts, chopped

Toss the chicken, kumquats, watercress and onions with the vinaigrette. Sprinkle on the chopped walnuts to serve. Serves 6–8.

*The chicken breasts are nicer if they have been marinated in a combination of oil, lime juice, garlic and a drop or two of lime oil before broiling.

This salad can be carried, already dressed, to the picnic.

For some reason I can almost always buy kumquats in Cork, but friends in New York tell me they only ever see them around Christmas.

Walnut Lime Vinaigrette

$^1/_4$ cup walnut oil

2 drops lime oil

$1^1/_2$ tablespoons lime juice

$^1/_2$ teaspoon salt

$^1/_2$ teaspoon Dijon mustard

Wild Rice Salad

2–3 cups cooked wild rice*

1 cup thinly sliced white part of leek, lightly cooked

$^3/_4$ cup pecans, roughly broken

$^1/_2$ cup cubed and cooked carrot

$^1/_2$ cup chopped green onions

Shallot Vinaigrette

Toss all the ingredients with the vinaigrette. Serves 8.

* I cup of dry wild rice

This can be carried to a picnic already dressed. I sometimes add cubes of cooked chicken, ham, pork or lamb, and/or kumquats. The salad is better made with roasted carrots.

Cherry Tomato and Mozzarella Salad

2 cups red and yellow cherry tomatoes, halved or quartered

1 cup cubed mozzarella

fresh basil, roughly chopped

vinaigrette with pesto* added

Toss the tomatoes with the mozzarella and basil and put into a picnic container.
If a lot of juice has accumulated, drain it off, mix it with the vinaigrette, and then
pour it on the salad. Serves 4–6.

*I have come to prefer pesto without the pine nuts and cheese, so the sauce I now make is
just 2 cups packed fresh basil, 4 garlic cloves, $^1/_4$ cup olive oil and a bit of salt
(and probably shouldn't be called pesto at all).

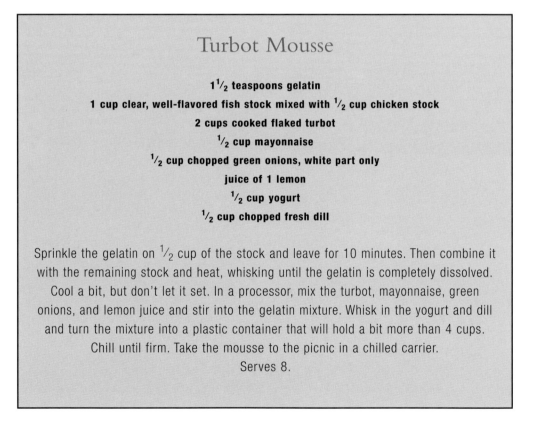

Turbot Mousse

1$^1/_2$ teaspoons gelatin

1 cup clear, well-flavored fish stock mixed with $^1/_2$ cup chicken stock

2 cups cooked flaked turbot

$^1/_2$ cup mayonnaise

$^1/_2$ cup chopped green onions, white part only

juice of 1 lemon

$^1/_2$ cup yogurt

$^1/_2$ cup chopped fresh dill

Sprinkle the gelatin on $^1/_2$ cup of the stock and leave for 10 minutes. Then combine it
with the remaining stock and heat, whisking until the gelatin is completely dissolved.
Cool a bit, but don't let it set. In a processor, mix the turbot, mayonnaise, green
onions, and lemon juice and stir into the gelatin mixture. Whisk in the yogurt and dill
and turn the mixture into a plastic container that will hold a bit more than 4 cups.
Chill until firm. Take the mousse to the picnic in a chilled carrier.
Serves 8.

There used to be a restaurant in Dublin called Snaffles. It was in a basement room decorated with hunting prints and dark wood. The waiters were typical old Dublin characters – our favorite always said "Look at that, then" when he brought the menus. We loved going there and miss it very much.

They served an appetizer that was delicious but quite rich, so I decided to use it as part of a picnic where one would take only a spoonful rather than an individual serving.

Mousse Like Snaffles Used to Make

6 oz. cream cheese, softened

$^3/_4$ cup jellied beef consommé

1 clove garlic pureed with a little salt

$^1/_2$ teaspoon curry powder

Process all ingredients together until smooth. Pour into a 2-cup plastic container and chill for two hours.

Another waterfall in County Kerry

Easter table

Table garden with wildflowers

(Facing) Christmas

Terrine of Two Salmons, Crab and Watercress

"Night and Day"

Parties

The restaurant business in country areas of Ireland is seasonal – ranging from extremely busy in the summer to practically no business at all in the winter. Because of this, our friends Marie and Gerry MacCloskey decided to close their wonderful restaurant in our village and open another near Shannon Airport. Gerry is an accomplished chef, and lovely, gentle Marie's fine taste was reflected in the prettiness of the restaurant. Her love of flowers often brought her to our garden and sent her foraging among the hedgerows, and the resulting arrangements made beautiful and unusual table settings. One idea of hers that I have never seen in another restaurant is to put an arrangement on each end of a long table.

We decided to give them a going away party with about thirty guests. It had to be a buffet, which meant I couldn't do special table settings. However, for Marie particularly, I wanted to create a memorable presentation, and finally came up with the idea of doing one look for dinner and a different one for desserts. We encouraged everyone to take their plates upstairs to the sitting room. As soon as I was fairly sure they all had any second helpings and fresh drinks they might want, I scurried like a fiend to and from the walk-in closet adjacent to the dining room, where I had stashed all the desserts except the ice cream, and managed to alter everything without anyone seeing it happen – including Richard! When everyone was called down to coffee and dessert, the table that had been covered with a blue and white cloth and rustic brown pottery was now all lace, crystal and silver. Later Marie told me she had expected magic once but not twice.

Despite the "Force-9" gale raging outside, the truly wonderful party ended with everyone dancing upstairs until 3 a.m.

The main dishes on the menu were fairly simple: chicken and mushroom crepes and a ground beef casserole. I chose the crepes because they can be frozen, and the casserole seemed a suitable meaty addition. I had chopped steamed radishes because they look pretty (but mainly as a result of letting them grow too big) and the zucchini because, as usual, we had too many in the garden. There was not much food left over, but what I did have I recycled into fresh dishes for houseguests we were expecting two days later. Most of the dishes had been garnished with chopped parsley or other herbs. I always ask guests if there is anything they don't eat, but wasn't worried this time because there were quite a few different things. How could I have anticipated that the reply to my question would be "I can't eat anything that has green specks on it"?

The party menu was:

CRUDITES WITH HONEY, GARLIC AND ORANGE MAYONNAISE* •
SMOKED SALMON PATE* • MUSHROOM AND NUT PATE* •
MIXED COLD SHELLFISH PLATTER *

* * *

CHICKEN AND MUSHROOM CREPES* • SPICED CAPONATA* •
GROUND BEEF AND NOODLE CASSEROLE* • CHOPPED RADISH
SALAD • TOMATOES WITH PESTO VINAIGRETTE • MARINATED
GREEN* AND YELLOW ZUCCHINI • BAKED RATTE POTATOES
WITH SOUR CREAM AND CHIVES

The desserts were:

PINEAPPLE CHEESECAKE • CHOCOLATE CHIP COOKIES •
CHOCOLATE BROWNIES • CHOCOLATE TRUFFLES • APPLE AND
HUCKLEBERRY CRISP • CHOCOLATE, STRAWBERRY AND
BUTTERSCOTCH ICE CREAM SUNDAES

Lunch in the conservatory

Chicken and Mushroom Crepes

For crepes:

12 eggs

3 cups flour

4 cups milk

³/₄ cup oil

¹/₂ teaspoon salt

butter for cooking crepes

Beat the eggs and add flour and milk, alternating and beating between each addition. Whisk in oil and salt and let stand for one hour. The batter should be the consistency of heavy cream. Melt a little butter in a 6-inch skillet, pour in a coffee measure (about ¹/₈ cup) of batter, and cook over medium heat, turning over to lightly brown other side. Stack and put aside. Makes about 50 crepes.

For filling:

3 lbs. button mushrooms, thinly sliced

butter

2 chickens, 3–4 lbs. each, cooked and cut into small pieces

8 tablespoons butter

8 tablespoons flour

2 pints warm chicken stock

2 cups warm milk

salt and pepper

¹/₄ cup dry sherry

Sauté the mushrooms in as little butter as possible and mix with the chicken pieces. Melt the 8 tablespoons butter, stir in the flour, and whisk in the stock and milk. Cook, stirring, until thickened, and add salt, pepper and sherry. Combine most of the sauce with chicken and mushrooms, saving enough to spoon between layers. Put a good spoonful of filling off-center on a crepe, roll up and place in a large ovenproof dish. Spoon a little sauce on each layer. If freezing, do not put the richer topping sauce on the crepes until just before serving.

Topping sauce:

6 tablespoons butter

6 tablespoons flour

2 cups warm chicken stock

2 cups warm cream

salt and pepper

3–4 tablespoons dry sherry

chopped parsley

Melt butter, stir in flour, and then whisk in the stock and cream. Cook, stirring, until thickened, and add salt, pepper and sherry to taste. Stir in some of the parsley. Pour sauce on top of crepes and bake in a 350° oven for 15 minutes or until just heated through. Sprinkle parsley on top.

Spiced Caponata

3 eggplants

salt

about $^1/_2$ cup fruity olive oil

4 onions, chopped

8 garlic cloves, chopped

5 celery stalks, chopped

2 cups pitted medium black olives, halved

10 plum tomatoes, peeled, seeded and chopped

$^1/_2$ cup capers, rinsed

$1^1/_2$ tablespoons sugar

$^1/_2$ cup red wine vinegar

$1^1/_2$ teaspoons cinnamon

1 teaspoon ground cardamom

Cut eggplants into $^3/_4$-inch slices (I don't peel them), salt, and drain on paper towels for 30 minutes. Rinse, dry, and cut the slices into cubes. Put the cubes in a bowl and toss them with just enough olive oil to lightly coat them. Sauté them, stirring until softened. Do the same with onions, garlic and celery. Mix in eggplant and all remaining ingredients and simmer, covered, for five minutes and uncovered for five more minutes. Refrigerate the caponata for at least one day, and serve at room temperature.

Once when I was making this, the only sugar I could find was cinnamon sugar, so I used it and have included cinnamon (and then cardamom) ever since.

Ground Beef and Noodle Casserole

1$\frac{1}{2}$ lbs. lean ground beef

1 tablespoon oil

1$\frac{1}{2}$ cups of tomato sauce

8 oz. light cream cheese, softened

$\frac{1}{2}$ cup sour cream

8 oz. lowfat cottage cheese, whipped (or ricotta cheese)

$\frac{1}{4}$ cup chopped green onions, mostly white parts

8 oz. fine pasta noodles, cooked and tossed with butter or oil

Lightly brown the beef in the oil, drain off extra fat, and stir in tomato sauce.
Mix together the cream cheese, sour cream, cottage cheese and onions. Put half
of the noodles in a lightly oiled casserole, then spread on all of the cheese and sour
cream mixture and the rest of the noodles. Spoon meat on top and bake, covered,
at 350° for 45 minutes (or longer at a lower temperature).

For one seafood luncheon for eighteen that we gave in honor of Marcia and
Tom Mitchell, visiting from the States, I set up two tables for nine on the
terrace, and to be sure all the guests had arrived, Marcia offered to take a
head count – luckily – because there were nineteen! There was no unexpected
guest – I think I just forgot to count myself.

The menu on that occasion, for which (luckily) I had prepared enough for at
least twenty, was:

SMOKED SALMON AND BROWN BREAD • CRAB CLAWS • COLD
LOBSTER AND PRAWNS WITH DILL SAUCE* • MUSSEL AND
TOMATO MOLD* • CEVICHE OF SQUID AND SCALLOPS* • MIXED
GREEN AND HERB SALAD WITH SHALLOT VINAIGRETTE* •
RHUBARB CRUMBLE CAKE*

We always buy crab claws from Cyril, our postman, not only because he
prepares them beautifully, but because he delivers them with the mail.

We are lucky to be able to buy lobster from local fishermen, and I always cook
them myself in sea water. This time, however, I bought them from a fisherman
whose wife insists on cooking them for his customers – at no extra cost,
which was a great help since I was using so many.

Mussel and Tomato Mold

5 tablespoons gelatin

2 cups mussel liquor

4 pints tomato or tomato/vegetable juice, heated

4 cups chopped mussels

1 cup Greek yogurt or light sour cream

1 cup plain yogurt

1 cup mayonnaise

$^1/_2$ cup chopped shallots or green onions

2 cups chopped, peeled and seeded tomatoes

juice of 2 lemons

Sprinkle the gelatin on the mussel liquor, leave for 10 minutes, and then pour on heated tomato juice, whisking to dissolve. Cool. Combine the mussels, yogurts, mayonnaise, shallots (or onions), tomatoes and lemon juice; whisk this into the gelatin mixture and turn it into two wet 8-cup molds. Chill until firm.

One of these molds would probably be enough for 18–20 people as part of a buffet, but I make two so it won't look skimpy when the last guests are serving themselves. I also like being able to use two different shapes.

Ceviche of Squid and Scallops

2 lbs. squid, cut in $^1/_2$ inch pieces

2 lbs. scallops, cut in $^1/_2$-inch pieces

2 cups lime juice

a few drops of lime oil

a few drops of hot pepper sauce

6 shallots, finely chopped

$^1/_2$ cup chopped cilantro (fresh coriander)

$^1/_4$ cup green coriander seed

Mix the squid, scallops, lime juice, oil and hot pepper sauce and leave to marinate in the refrigerator for 1–3 days, stirring daily (be sure all the fish is covered with lime juice). Before serving, mix in the shallots, cilantro and coriander seed.

Richard doesn't like squid so sometimes I make the ceviche with other whitefish instead. Actually, come to think of it, he doesn't really like ceviche so I probably use other whitefish because it is easier to deal with than squid.

I pick green coriander seeds as soon as they form – they have an entirely different flavor from the dried ones. Even though I plant the slow-bolt variety at intervals from spring onward, lots of seedlings pop up as well, so I usually have some green seed to use.

Rhubarb Crumble Cake

Cake:

4 cups self-rising flour

2 teaspoons cinnamon

2 teaspoons baking powder

$3/4$ cup lightly packed brown sugar

12 oz. butter, cut in small pieces

2 eggs, beaten with $1/2$ teaspoon vanilla and 5 tablespoons milk

Filling:

12 oz. (about 3 cups) rhubarb, cut in $1/2$-inch pieces

6–7 tablespoons brown sugar

1 teaspoon cinnamon

In a processor mix all the dry ingredients, put the pieces of butter on top, and process on and off until the mixture looks like bread crumbs. Take out 2 rounded cups and put them aside for the crumble topping. Add the eggs, vanilla, and milk and process to make a soft dough.
Oil the bottom and sides of an 8-inch springform baking pan and spread the dough evenly over the pan, indenting it a little towards the middle. (If the dough is sticky, I wet my fingers to help spread it.) Mix together the rhubarb, sugar, and cinnamon, spoon onto the dough, pressing it down lightly, and sprinkle the reserved crumble over the top. Bake at 350° for $1 1/4$–$1 1/2$ hours until the top is brown. Cool on a wire rack. The cake can also be frozen.

One summer Frankie and four other friends, Jerry, Marie, Derry and Dorothy, were turning forty, and since we had long thought we should show our appreciation for being made so welcome in the community, we decided to have a party for them to jointly celebrate the occasions. The invitations read that we were celebrating the collective 200 years of the honorees.

Planning any outdoor event in Ireland is always risky, so we hoped to hire a big yellow and white striped tent which – because there had been posters around advertising the circus – inspired talk that the show had come to our lower pasture!

The plan was to start with drinks in the garden and move on to the tent for dinner, but we did have a bad-weather alternative. If the worst happened we would jam everyone into the house for drinks and then dash with umbrellas to the lower field. There was no plan if the absolute worst happened and a gale blew the tent into the bay.

It was the boys' first gig . . . alternating with canned music played by our electrician, who had brought lighting effects from the disco he runs at the parish hall.

One can now find elegant looking tents (known here as "marquees") complete with flooring, but, apart from the white and yellow stripes, our tent was more country-serviceable than festive. To make a dance floor, we nailed thick plywood onto milk-container pallets borrowed from the creamery. The church lent us tables, and the school supplied benches. For live music we hired fifteen-year-old Liam Mulvaney's newly formed band. It was the boys' first gig and they were terrific, alternating with canned music played by our electrician, who had brought lighting effects from the disco he runs at the parish hall.

Because it was the season of long days, we could avoid the hazard of candlelight during dinner, but when it finally began to get dark, Richard switched on battery lamps he had placed on each table. We found the lamps quite by accident in Cork, but apparently no one had seen them before, and it amused us to see how startled everyone was when suddenly it became light as Richard walked by each table and casually snapped on the lamps.

Things are seldom easy in the Irish countryside. I wanted to use plain, bright-colored helium balloons tied to the backs of all the chairs, and it never occurred to me that finding them might present a problem, but when I called the only local balloon supplier he said we'd have to see to the helium ourselves, and did I want the ones with Tweety Bird or the ones with Bugs Bunny? In the end we had a friend send plain ones from London and drove to a small town 100 miles away for the helium.

Even though our estimated guest count was just over 100, I wanted to do all the food myself, with only some last-day help from Frankie. As always, however, I did accept offers of desserts, and when one of the guests insisted on contributing something, I said a large potato salad would be welcome. He forgot.

A month ahead of the party date I set about making things that could be frozen, which were mostly the hors d'oeuvres. As many of the dishes could be made a few days in advance, the major part of the preparations took up the whole week preceding the party. I enjoyed it immensely and learned much, but it was a lot of work and I'm afraid poor Richard had to fend pretty much for himself during the process.

The party lasted well into dawn, and early the next morning when the crew came to take down the tent (it was booked for Maureen O'Hara's golf tournament), we had only just cleaned up the last of the debris. We were exhausted, but it was worth all the effort and our only regret was the emptiness of the pasture. The circus had gone.

A postscript on marquees: when our friend Peggy needed a tent for her daughter's wedding reception, she arranged it through the same company we had used. She was away when the tent was set up, its yellow and white striped canvas very upmarket this time, and when she returned, Peggy was happily impressed until she went inside and found it smelled strongly of the livestock which it had housed at a country fair a few days earlier. Following threats of tantrums, a less pungent replacement was installed only shortly before the Italian groom's family arrived from Rome. Just about all the village population turned out to watch the variety of amazing hats and other Italian high fashion arriving at the church but, for us, the most memorable moment was seeing the bride at the reception, with the sea as a backdrop, chatting with three nuns who had been her teachers.

Party Menu for 100

HORS D'OEUVRES

CHARD AND MUSHROOM ROULADE* • SMOKED SALMON MOUSSE* ON GREEN ONION WAFFLES* • CRUDITES WITH HERBED MAYONNAISE • COUNTRY TERRINE WITH PISTACHIOS* • MINCED HAM SALAD WITH TORTILLA CHIPS • TUNA PATE • MUSHROOMS MARINATED WITH CUMIN AND CORIANDER* • CRAB CLAWS AND PRAWNS

COLD BUFFET

ROAST TENDERLOINS OF BEEF • WHOLE SALMONS* WITH DILL SAUCE* AND LEMON MAYONNAISE • STUFFED VINE LEAVES* • CHINESE CHICKEN SALAD* • PASTA, TOMATO AND PESTO SALAD • ROASTED RED AND YELLOW PEPPERS • MUSSELS TOPPED WITH ORZO SALAD* • MIXED COOKED VEGETABLES VINAIGRETTE • MAUI ONION, ORANGE, BEET, ENDIVE AND WATERCRESS SALAD • OYSTERS

The **tuna paté** is just plain old tuna salad with onions and pickle relish, but mixing it in the processor using the plastic blade makes it more of a paté. Ham salad is simple also – ready-cooked picnic ham minced in the processor and mixed with relish and mayonnaise. The crab claws as always came from Cyril who, with his wife, was also a guest. It was too early in the year for me to have enough basil for the pesto, but I did have quite a lot frozen from the previous year. Maui onions are definitely not an Irish crop, but I had smuggled a few back on a visit to the States in May. (Now we grow Walla Walla onions and I don't have to smuggle.) Philippe supplied and, thank goodness, opened the oysters.

PARTY PLAN COUNTDOWN:

One month ahead: Make roulade and freeze.

One month or three weeks ahead: Make waffles, terrines and stuffed vine leaves. Freeze.

Two weeks ahead: Marinate mushrooms.

FINAL WEEK:

Monday: Make mayonnaise and other dressings.

Tuesday: Roast peppers and onions. Cook and freeze mussels.

Wednesday: Cook chickens, beets, and beef tenderloins pastas. Slice oranges. Blanch and peel tomatoes.

Thursday: Cook cauliflower, carrots, broccoli and leeks. Chop tomatoes. Make smoked salmon mousse. Cook and trim salmon. Make vinaigrette. Shred beets. Take terrines from freezer to fridge. Cook pastas.

Friday: Arrange peppers, slice and arrange beef. Top and tail beans. Slice terrines and arrange on platters. Make orzo salad. Take quiche, waffles, vine leaves and mussels from freezer to fridge. Make tuna salad. Make ham salad.

Saturday: Dress chicken salad and put on platter. Cook beans. Make pasta salad and put on platter. Chop and mix vegetables. Mix chives into cream cheese for roulade.

Sunday: Fill, roll, and cut roulade. Crisp waffles and pipe on salmon. Mix vegetable salad. Mix Maui onion salad. Cut vegetables for crudités. Pipe mousse onto waffles. Arrange anything left onto serving pieces. Lie down.

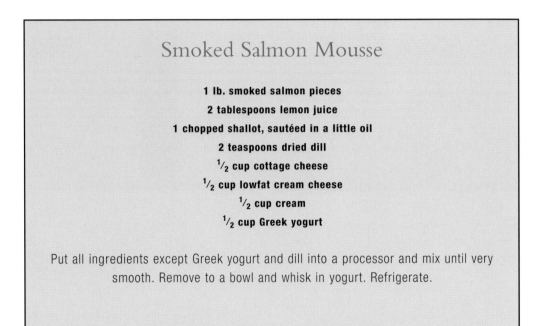

Smoked Salmon Mousse

1 lb. smoked salmon pieces

2 tablespoons lemon juice

1 chopped shallot, sautéed in a little oil

2 teaspoons dried dill

$^1/_2$ cup cottage cheese

$^1/_2$ cup lowfat cream cheese

$^1/_2$ cup cream

$^1/_2$ cup Greek yogurt

Put all ingredients except Greek yogurt and dill into a processor and mix until very smooth. Remove to a bowl and whisk in yogurt. Refrigerate.

Green Onion Waffles

5$\frac{1}{2}$ cups Bisquick baking mix

4 tablespoons oil

2 eggs

2$\frac{1}{2}$ cups milk

2 cups very finely chopped green onions

sprigs of fresh dill

In a processor mix all ingredients until smooth. Let stand for 30 minutes and pour onto a hot waffle griddle. If the waffles are being made for freezing, take them off slightly underdone and cut them into 1-inch squares. Makes about 140.
When ready to assemble waffles, put squares in 300° oven to crisp for 15 minutes, cool a little, and, with a pastry bag, pipe on Smoked Salmon Mousse. Top each square with a sprig of fresh dill. Makes enough for about 125 squares.

Country Terrine with Pistachios

$\frac{1}{2}$ lb. each of chicken livers, ground pork and ground veal

1 large onion, chopped and lightly sautéed in a little oil

3 oz. ground pork fat

$\frac{1}{4}$ lb. smoked ham, diced

$\frac{1}{2}$ cup heavy cream

$\frac{1}{4}$ cup cognac

$\frac{1}{4}$ cup roughly chopped pistachio nuts

2 eggs, beaten

3 garlic cloves, chopped

$\frac{1}{2}$ teaspoon each of allspice and mace

pinch of ground cloves

1 teaspoon salt

Puree the chicken livers and mix in all remaining ingredients. Spoon into two heavy rectangular 6-cup terrines, and put these in a roasting pan. Pour in hot water to come halfway up sides of terrines and bake, covered, at 350°. Uncover and continue baking until they reach a temperature of 190°. Cool, covered with foil, putting some weights on top. The flavor is better after refrigerating a few days. They can also be frozen.

For the party I tripled the recipe. I will never forget facing all those pureed livers, first thing, on the morning I made the terrines!

Mushrooms Marinated with Cumin and Coriander

$1\frac{1}{2}$ lbs. clean, small, tightly closed mushrooms

2 pints water

2 tablespoons sea salt

$\frac{1}{2}$ cup white wine vinegar and 1/4 cup red wine vinegar

$2\frac{1}{2}$ tablespoons cumin seed

1 tablespoon coriander seed, cracked

1 teaspoon white peppercorns, cracked

1 teaspoon sugar

2 bay leaves, a cinnamon stick, a pinch of thyme and a sprig of rosemary

2 garlic cloves, bruised

olive oil

Boil the mushrooms in water with 1 tablespoon of the salt. Drain and cool mushrooms, saving a scant cup of the water, and boil the remaining ingredients, except the garlic and olive oil, in the liquid for three minutes. Cool. Put the mushrooms in a large jar that has a secure lid and pour them over the liquid mixture. Add garlic and enough olive oil to cover mushrooms. Keep jar in a cool place and turn over daily for at least 10 days.

Being able to buy fresh wild salmon is one of the joys of living on the coast of Ireland. The salmon-fishing season is short and strictly monitored, so when the fish is plentiful and the price is at its lowest, we all buy as much as we have room to freeze, as well as some to use fresh. The date the season begins varies up and down the coast, with our particular area being the earliest, so I was able to use fresh salmon for the party.

Most of the time I poach whole salmon in the fish kettle that I always borrow from Pat Mulvaney, but since I was cooking two this time, I did them both in the oven in turkey-size roasting bags.

Being able to buy fresh wild salmon is one of the joys of living on the coast of Ireland.

Whole Salmon in a Roasting Bag

1 lemon
a 7- or 8-lb. salmon, cleaned, head left on
2 leeks
$^1/_2$ onion, quartered

Squeeze lemon juice on salmon and into cavity. Save lemon halves. Trim leeks, cut down one side of outermost layers, separating so that you have quite a few long, wide pieces. Cut the rest in half lengthwise. Put a roasting bag on a baking tray. Crosswise, lay in the wide leek pieces, put the salmon on top, and place cut lemon and onion in its cavity. Lay rest of leeks around and on top of the salmon. Close bag, cut a few holes in it, and bake the fish at 350° for 60–80 minutes (or about 10–12 minutes per pound, cleaned weight).

Open bag and as soon as fish can be handled, peel away top skin, and, with a spatula, following the grain, scrape off brown bits. Pull leeks from under the fish and lay them on top of the flesh to prevent it from drying out. Drain away juices from the roasting bag and lift the bag onto a large piece of plastic wrap. Cut away top half of bag, and if it will come away easily, pull it from under the fish; if not, trim it closely, wrap plastic around fish, and refrigerate. The plastic and any remaining bag can be tucked out of sight under the fish after it is on a platter.

The hotter the fish, the easier it is to skin it and pull away leeks and bag. I wear tight-fitting rubber gloves for skinning, but I need to use bare hands for the scraping in order not to be clumsy and make a mess of it.

If I am cooking a defrosted salmon, I wrap it in seaweed and then put it on the leeks. Wrapping a previously frozen fish in seaweed may or may not produce a better result, but I get enormous satisfaction from walking down to our beach to gather the weed from the tide pools, and I am convinced — probably because I want to be — that the seaweed method makes it less possible to detect the difference between a fresh and a frozen fish. For the same reason I freeze whole fish intact rather than gutting them.

Stuffed Vine Leaves

1¹/₂ cups chopped green onions

¹/₂ cup olive oil

³/₄ cup uncooked long-grain rice

1 15-oz. can Italian tomatoes, pureed

1 lb. ground lean lamb

3 cups chopped fresh mint

2 tablespoons fresh rosemary, chopped

¹/₄ cup pine nuts, lightly toasted

¹/₄ cup dried currants

40 vine leaves in brine, thoroughly rinsed

juice of 1 lemon

Sauté the onions in olive oil until just soft, then add rice, pureed tomatoes and 1 cup of water. Cover and simmer for 15 minutes. Mix in all the rest of the ingredients, except the lemon, and simmer until the lamb is done. Put about a tablespoon of the filling on the veined side of each leaf; roll up, tucking in sides; and set them seam side down, in layers, in a heavy pot. Pour lemon juice over top and add enough water to just barely cover. Weight down the leaves and simmer, covered, for one hour. Cool, then remove the parcels from the liquid. Serve at room temperature.

The vine leaves freeze very well. I tripled the recipe for the party.

Chinese Chicken Salad

2 3-lb. chickens, cooked

2 cups canned or fresh baby corn

1 lb. snow peas, blanched

2 cups bean sprouts

2 cups roughly chopped water chestnuts

3 tablespoons rinsed and chopped preserved ginger

Salad dressing:

2¹/₂ cups mayonnaise

2 tablespoons light soy sauce

2 tablespoons lemon juice

2 teaspoons chili paste with garlic

1 teaspoon sesame oil

1 teaspoon Chinese five-spice powder

Take chicken meat off the bones and shred it into 1¹/₂-inch pieces. Slice corn in half lengthwise and toss all salad ingredients together. Mix dressing and spoon onto the salad, tossing until it is nicely coated – it may not be necessary to use all the dressing. This will make enough for 30 people as part of a buffet.

For the party I doubled the recipe using six chickens, squashing three together in two turkey-size roasting bags, so that with one parcel in each oven I was able to get the lot done at one time.

Mussels Topped with Orzo Salad

40 cooked mussels

$^3/_4$ cup orzo pasta, cooked

$^1/_4$ cup roasted and chopped yellow pepper

$^1/_4$ cup chopped, skinned and seeded tomato

$^1/_4$ cup chopped flat-leaf parsley

2 tablespoons chopped chives

$^1/_4$ cup finely chopped smoked ham

Shallot Vinaigrette

Remove the mussels from their shells, keeping 40 half shells. Make sure the mussels are completely debearded and rinse them. Combine all the ingredients for the topping and toss them with Shallot Vinaigrette. Put the mussels on their shells and top with a teaspoon of orzo mixture.

I tripled the recipe (plus a little), freezing 150 cooked mussels for less than a week. Knowing that freezing them short term wouldn't affect the flavor or texture gave me the great advantage of being able to get the cooking and shelling out of the way well in advance.

We recently tried cooking some mussels that had been frozen, uncooked, in their shells and vacuum packed. They really weren't very good at all – the ones frozen after cooking are much better.

For years I've wanted to line the beams on the ceiling of the dining room with greenery for Christmas. I knew it would be a BIG undertaking, but finally this past December 21, we did it (the "we" being Ava and Richard, and Steve and Eileen who look after our garden).

Steve's most important part in this project was to steadfastly refuse all summer long to prune the cypress trees in another garden he tends because he knew I needed that particular greenery for Christmas. It keeps well and it wouldn't drop needles onto our "dress up" dinner on the twenty-fourth, or our party for fifty-odd on the twenty-seventh.

Richard did the initial stapling up of eighteen two-inch strips of chicken wire which I had cut the night before. The next day, while I was in Cork collecting our friend Lynda who came from London for the holidays, he filled in some spaces where wire showed through the greenery. I did all the rest – with a great deal of help from Eileen.

After the chicken wire was up, next came the lights. I had brought two strings of 250 from the States because they are more delicate looking, and much less expensive than the Irish or English lights. They do, however, require transformers because of the 220 voltage. Fortunately we have several; unfortunately, although I made sure all lights worked when I unpacked them, fifty on each strand didn't work when they were up. No chance of replacement in Ireland so I just had to cut out the dead ones and rewire the strings. Once the lights were up AND working, Eileen sorted the greens into suitable fronds and I stuck them through the wire and adjusted the lights. It took many, many trips up and down the ladder, and a full day to put up – but it was worth the effort, particularly because the dining room is also the entry to the house, so the greens and lights were the first thing anyone coming in would see.

After collecting Lynda from the airport, there were two very important things on my agenda: lobsters for the Christmas Eve mixed seafood main course, and a small Christmas tree. Lobster has never been difficult to get – except, apparently, this December. The fish man who comes to the house couldn't get any. No one in Cork had any.

Small Christmas trees ARE difficult to get. We stopped at every single nursery and flower shop we saw – every tree was too big. Even if they were cut down, all were still too tall to be put on the table in the window in the upstairs sitting room. Eventually we made one last stop at a fish shop I had been told did have lobsters (they had been seen swimming in a tank). Indeed, they were swimming in a tank – but they were reserved for someone else. I finally decided I'd have to use monkfish instead. Having bought the fish and a few extra prawns, we left the shop and practically fell over the only small Christmas tree for sale in the West of Ireland.

Although there were only the three of us that evening, I made our traditional sausage and lentil tree-trimming dinner which was originally devised to fill up growing boys and their friends, but the adults have always happily devoured it as well.

Sausage and Lentils

1 cup green lentils

$^1/_2$ cup chopped onion

1–2 garlic cloves, chopped

a 15-oz. can chopped Italian tomatoes

1 tablespoon olive oil

1 teaspoon sugar

2 teaspoons thyme

a bay leaf

1$^1/_2$ lbs. kielbasa-type sausages, skinned and cut into chunks

Rinse the lentils and then simmer them for 20 minutes in water to cover by at least an inch. Drain and keep any liquid that may be left. Sauté onions and garlic in the oil until just softened. Stir in the tomatoes, sugar, thyme and bay leaf. Simmer for 10 minutes and then add the sausages, lentils and enough liquid (I use wine) to just barely cover, and simmer for a further 20–30 minutes.

The next day we stopped in to see our friend, Gene, who teaches French and English and is married to a fisherman. While we were having a glass of wine, the door opened and there stood her husband, Denis Joseph – known as "Dinjo" – framed in the doorway, holding sacks of shellfish in each hand. His fierce black beard contrasted with a dripping, bright-yellow hooded slicker and dark-green Wellington boots. He was majestic. Exuding the fresh, overpowering smell of the ocean, he seemed to have brought the sea right into the house. It was a magical moment. It was also the solution to my lobster dilemma. Of course Dinjo would be able to get me what I needed. The cats got the monkfish. It was Christmas after all.

With lobster back on the menu, I was ready to get on with the cooking. The rest of the seafood had been frozen for a very short time, slightly undercooked, in its sauce before adding cream. During the summer, autumn and in mid-December, I had frozen quite a lot of things I needed for both Christmas Eve and the party three days later, so the last hours of preparation were relatively easy.

I always grow white beets and a variety called "chioggia" that comes in various shades of pink and pinky orange. They have a wonderful flavor and are useful in salads, or mixed with other vegetables, because they don't bleed. In August I made plenty of white borscht and froze it along with some cooked and pureed bright pink chioggias. Also, from the garden, I froze tomatoes for sauce, ruby chard, basil, and lots of blueberries.

Frankie made a cheesecake for Richard's birthday. Her cheesecake is very light, but Richard didn't know that, so I convinced him he needed to lose a few pounds and promptly froze it to have along with our traditional Oatmeal Christmas Pudding.

The shredded squash and lobsters I did in the morning and the rice in the afternoon, so the main part of the evening's work was just reheating. Actually, I always try to get most of the cooking done somewhat in advance, but this time I think I worked it out better than usual – probably because I didn't want to be in the kitchen while everyone else was having champagne and caviar along with the wonderful chicken merguez sausages, brought back from France especially to use for Christmas – an unlikely but (as it turned out) popular addition to the caviar.

Richard and I really like to dress up for Christmas Eve, so we requested our guests to wear evening clothes, and it wasn't until he was dressing for dinner himself that Richard discovered that not only were all his formal shirts yellowed from disuse, but he couldn't find a black tie or even an acceptable alternative. I can't fault his substitution of a red velvet smoking jacket and a cravat with his tuxedo trousers, but neither of us remembered he ever had such a thing, and where it came from remains a mystery.

Remembering the success of the MacCloskeys' going-away party, when I managed to change the table appearance between dinner and dessert, I wanted some sort of a surprise again. None of our Christmas Eve guests other than Lynda knew how we had decorated the dining room, and we hoped to save the full effect until dinnertime. Fortunately everyone arrived together, because Richard allowed only a glimpse of the room with the greenery – very dimly lit – while they were quickly stripped of their topcoats and all but pushed upstairs to the sitting room. When it was time to come to the table, our guests could see candlelight, but we waited until they were all nearly down the stairs before we snapped on the overhead Christmas lights among the pine branches. To my delight, someone said that it was like dining in a grotto.

Christmas Eve dinner for ten:

WHITE BEET BORSCHT WITH PINK BEET CREAM[*] • LOBSTER, SHRIMPS, SCALLOPS AND SALMON IN GINGERED TOMATO SAUCE[*] • BASMATI RICE • SHREDDED GREEN AND YELLOW SQUASH WITH GARLIC AND BASIL • RUBY CHARD • MIXED WINTER GREEN SALAD • CHEESECAKE WITH BLUEBERRY SAUCE • OATMEAL CHRISTMAS PUDDING[*]

White Beet Borscht with Pink Beet Cream

2 lbs. white beets

2 medium onions

1 medium parsnip

1 medium cabbage, whitest part only

2 leeks, white part only

4 pints light chicken stock

a bay leaf

juice of 1 lemon

salt and white pepper

a bright pink beet, cooked and pureed

$1/2$ cup sour cream

Peel and chop all the vegetables. Soften the onion in a little stock, then add the rest of the vegetables, bay leaf and stock, and simmer for about $1^1/_2$ hours. Remove bay leaf, cool the soup, and puree it in a processor. It should not be perfectly smooth. Add lemon juice and salt and pepper to taste. Combine the pink beet puree and sour cream. Reheat soup and serve with a spoonful of sour cream mixture swirled on top. Serves at least 10.

The soup freezes very well, as does the beet puree. I grow yellow beets as well as the white and pink ones, so I sometimes garnish white borscht with swirls of yellow beet cream or a mix of pink and yellow – or pink borscht with white and yellow – or yellow with . . .

Lobster, Shrimps, Scallops and Salmon
in Gingered Tomato Sauce

3 medium lobster tails

25 shrimps

15 large scallops

white wine

8 oz. salmon fillet

25 plum tomatoes

20 sun-dried tomatoes

3 shallots, chopped

1 pint light vegetable stock

1 tablespoon grated ginger

1 cup orange juice

1 cup cream

Cook lobsters and shrimps in sea water – be careful not to overcook. Cut lobster into chunks. Slice scallops in half crosswise and poach in enough white wine to just cover until still slightly opaque – about a minute. Cut salmon into two pieces and poach in white wine until almost done – about three minutes. Set all the seafood aside.
Peel and thoroughly deseed plum tomatoes.
Chop sun-dried tomatoes as finely as possible. Soften shallots in a little stock and then add the tomatoes, ginger, orange juice and remaining stock.
Simmer for 20–30 minutes, cool and puree as smoothly as possible.
To serve, stir cream into sauce, add seafood and reheat very gently.
Serves 10.

Because the ocean is on our doorstep, I always cook lobsters and shrimps in sea water and have learned that it is a good idea to keep a large bottle of it in the larder in case the tide is low or the weather terrible when I need it.

I had experimented with freezing this dish on another occasion so I knew it would work. I froze all the seafood (except lobster this time) for just a week, completely covered in sauce, and then defrosted it overnight in the fridge. I hadn't used salmon before, but that is the only fishy thing that our friend Declan eats, and it was a fine addition. Undercooking slightly is a good idea because the sauce does have to be very hot in order to reheat and everything gets a little more done.

C_____l Christmas Pudding

cups sifted all-purpose flour

1$^1/_2$ cups sugar

2 teaspoons baking soda

2 teaspoons ground cinnamon

2 cups dried oats

1$^1/_2$ cups raisins

2$^1/_2$ cups buttermilk

6 tablespoons melted butter

1 tablespoon vanilla

Grease a 1 quart pudding basin or mixing bowl. Into a large bowl sift together the flour, sugar, baking soda and cinnamon, and stir in the oatmeal and raisins. Combine the buttermilk, melted butter and vanilla; and pour onto flour mixture, beating well, and then pour into pudding basin. Cover the basin with a double thickness of foil, tie it securely, and put in a steamer with enough water to come halfway up basin. Steam for about two hours or until a knife inserted in pudding comes out clean or fairly clean – pudding will be somewhat sticky. Unmold and wrap in foil. Keep in fridge for 2–3 weeks or much longer frozen. Reheat, wrapped in foil, in a slow oven.

We hadn't given a large party for a long time, so, because of the dining room decorations this seemed the right time to do it. The invitations read, "Drinks and snacks from 5 until 8."

Because no one pays much attention to RSVP-ing here and the weather was stormy, we didn't know how many to expect. However, nearly everyone turned up and, in the Irish way, it was the usual eclectic mixture with their mates: the electrician, the cheesemaker, the vet, various farmers, the police sergeant, the postman, a count and countess, the doctor, the school principal, Gene and Dinjo, Steve and Eileen, a lord and lady, a Yale professor of dramaturgy, an English cinematographer with his film makeup artist girlfriend and their producer houseguest, the chairman of Aer Lingus, the realtors and, briefly, a couple of restaurateurs in chef garb because they had to get back to work.

Drinks were set up in the small conservatory off the dining room. We had a full bar as well as both red and white wine, but because of the oatmeal-colored carpets in the sitting room we put out only white wine up there. People were encouraged to wander anywhere with their drinks, of course, but guess who spilled the only red wine on the carpet? And it wasn't even from my own glass! The old white-wine-on-top-of-red trick erased the stain without a trace, however, so I didn't get yelled at. Just smirked at.

We didn't expect people to leave by 8, but we did think that by 10 o'clock there would be just us and the Neuberger family, who were arriving from London late in the evening. WRONG! At 10 there were more than a few stragglers, and after most of the food was gone, at 10:30 our young friend Liam from up the hill arrived with some members of his rock band and their girlfriends (the same band, grown up, who had their first "gig" at our tent party all those years ago). We didn't see them away until 2 a.m. The large quantity of chili con carne I had in the freezer saved the day.

There is a tradition at noon on Christmas Day that as many hearty souls who are brave enough – or crazy enough – swim for charity. This year it was sunny but freezing cold. The whole village was bundled up to watch from the pier. The doctor stood on the beach taking pictures, just in case, and another local handed around brandy when the swimmers came out. The fact that we all knew each other and were gathered together in such high spirits in this beautiful spot by the ocean on Christmas Day really was exhilarating. It was then that we received most of our acceptances for the party.

The snacks at the party for fifty to sixty were:

CRUSTLESS SPINACH QUICHE* • SAVORY ROSEMARY PASTRIES* • SAUSAGE BALLS IN MUSTARD SAUCE* • SMOKY DEVILED EGGS* • CRUDITES WITH CURRY MAYONNAISE • BRUSSELS SPROUTS IN BLUE CHEESE SAUCE* • ROASTED NEW POTATOES WITH SOUR CREAM AND CHIVES • WAFFLE SQUARES WITH PEPPERED CRABAPPLE JELLY AND CREAM CHEESE • DEEP-FRIED WALNUTS* • CHRISTMAS ROSES*

Since I had been able to freeze so much, again the preparation was quite easy. The quiche, tarts, sausage balls and waffles came from the freezer; the eggs must be cooked and marinated for up to eight days; Lynda prepared the crudités and arranged them in a wonderful checkerboard pattern; and I got the brussels sprouts at Marks & Spencer in Cork – washed and ready to cook. I've never forgotten a very fancy Beverly Hills party where the host had brussels sprouts as one of his many hors d'oeuvres, and because we love them I decided to have a bowlful. Although I didn't really think they'd be popular, they all went, and quite quickly, too. But then this is cabbage country.

Timmy O'Regan once told me that if you bury some of your first new potatoes in an airtight tin, they will keep until Christmas, and that is how we were able to have them for the party. It was Steve's assignment to remember just where in the garden we had buried them.

Crustless Spinach Quiche

- 1 large onion, chopped
- 2 large garlic cloves, chopped
- 2 tablespoons oil
- 2 lbs. frozen chopped spinach, defrosted and drained
- 1/2 cup sour cream
- 12 eggs, beaten
- 8 oz. Jarlsberg cheese, grated
- 2 teaspoons nutmeg
- salt and pepper
- 4 oz. grated Parmesan cheese

Sauté the onion and garlic in the oil until just softened. Mix with the spinach, sour cream, eggs, Jarlsberg cheese, nutmeg, a large pinch of salt and a good grinding of pepper. Pour into a greased 18 x 12–inch rimmed baking pan, and bake in a 350° oven for 20–25 minutes until set. Sprinkle with Parmesan and put back in the oven for a few minutes. Cool, and cut it into triangles. There will be about 90.

If frozen, they might get a bit soggy (especially if the spinach wasn't thoroughly drained), so reheat for quite a long time – but do keep watch. I burned the last batch, but that was mainly because I'd put them on the oven floor to speed things up.

About draining spinach and other greens: I lay the defrosted or fresh wet greens on a terry cloth towel, roll it up and press very hard. (Actually what I really do is roll it up and walk on it.) I keep dark green towels just for this purpose, so if they get stained it hardly shows.

Savory Rosemary Pastries

- 3 1/3 cups flour
- 1 cup olive oil
- 3/4 cup water
- 6 teaspoons fresh rosemary, chopped (4 teaspoons dried)
- 1/2 teaspoon salt and sea salt

In a processor mix together flour, oil, water, rosemary and salt until just combined. Press the dough into two rectangular pieces, wrap in plastic and put in fridge for an hour. Bring the dough to room temperature, and roll into 1/8-inch-thick rectangles. Place them on lightly oiled baking sheets, and, using a pastry wheel, cut them into 1-inch pastries (so they can be separated easily after baking) and sprinkle lightly with sea salt. Bake at 425° for 15–20 minutes. Cool.

The pastries can be frozen but are quite delicate, so pack carefully in layers in a rigid container. Defrost in fridge and reheat in a 350° oven for 15 minutes.

Sausage Balls in Mustard Sauce

5 lbs. lean ground pork

5 tablespoons sausage seasoning

1 tablespoon each English and Dijon mustard

2 tablespoons grainy mustard

1 cup sour cream

1 cup yogurt

Mix meat with seasoning, form into 70 balls, and put them on baking sheets in a 350° oven for 20 minutes, turning them over once. Mix the mustards with the sour cream and yogurt, add the sausage balls and slowly heat (but don't boil, or the yogurt will curdle).
The sausage balls freeze very well.

We have all sorts of wonderful sausages in Ireland, but I wanted to make some with the taste unique to American ones. Richard's brother, Mike, who is a butcher, gave me the seasoning in a 1-lb. package that says it is enough to do 50 lbs. I've written on it "1 tablespoon = 1 lb." so I guess that's how the arithmetic comes out.

Brussels Sprouts in Blue Cheese Sauce

3 lbs. brussels sprouts, washed and trimmed

chicken stock

8 oz. blue cheese

1 cup lowfat mayonnaise

$\frac{1}{2}$ cup yogurt

Boil sprouts in stock for eight or nine minutes – so they are still somewhat firm. Drain them thoroughly, and dry with a terry cloth towel. Stir cheese with mayonnaise in a heavy saucepan over gentle heat until cheese melts and then, off the heat, whisk in yogurt. Toss with warm sprouts and serve at room temperature.

For years I have cut a cross in the bottom of brussels sprouts, but this time since I bought them ready to cook, I forgot about it, and it didn't make any difference.

Deep-Fried Walnuts

4 cups walnuts
3 pints water
$^1/_2$ cup sugar
oil for deep frying
salt

Boil walnuts about one minute, rinse under hot water, drain, and then stir the warm nuts with the sugar until the sugar dissolves. In a frying basket, deep-fry the nuts in batches in 350° oil for about a minute, until brown but not burned. Drain on paper towels and sprinkle with a little salt.

Be sure to lower frying basket into oil very slowly or the fat may boil over. I sometimes add a teaspoon (or more) of curry, cumin or cinnamon to the sugar.

Christmas Roses

For the dough:
14 oz. butter
$^3/_4$ cup sugar
2 egg yolks
1 teaspoon vanilla extract
$3^3/_4$ cups flour

chopped hazelnuts
seedless raspberry jam

In a processor mix all dough ingredients until just combined. Turn out onto a floured board and knead a bit, adding more flour if dough is very sticky. Form the dough into balls the size of walnuts, roll them in the chopped nuts and put on nonstick baking sheets. With your thumb, make an indentation in center of each ball and spoon in a little raspberry jam. Bake in a 350° oven for 20 minutes. Makes 5 dozen.

A last note: I'd been dreading taking down all the greenery and lights, but surprisingly it was a much less difficult task than expected, and because the beams are stained wood, the staple marks aren't even visible. I actually managed all of the undoing, while Richard took Lynda back to the airport on January 2, and had the room cleaned and back to normal when he returned four hours later.

Harvesting
artichokes
(above) for
roses and
artichoke
centerpiece
(facing)

Table gardens
with garden
flowers

CHAPTER SEVEN

"Just the way you cook tonight"

At the Table

One of the things I most enjoy is planning table settings, and though finding
storage space is now becoming a problem, I've accumulated a good variety of
tableware, cloths, mats and napkins, none of which are very costly. I don't
have any "fine" china or crystal – except for ten Waterford wine glasses
purchased thirty years ago when I was visiting Aunt Dellie at Lismore Castle,
and two newer ones in supposedly the same pattern (which are quite

different, nowhere near the weight or quality of cutting, and cost twice as much). The only other really "good" things I put on the table are some lovely flatware and silver I inherited from my Great-Aunt Maud.

I like to use mostly brightly colored dinner plates along with plain or patterned smaller ones for salads and starters, and cloths or place mats in patterns and colors that fit in with the dishes. I also have several variations of blue and white. If we are eating outside, I pin small fishing weights to the corners of the cloth – they are unobtrusive and certainly help to keep the ends from blowing around. Most of my dinner plates are seconds, a few are inexpensive "antiques," and some of my favorites come from a DIY (Do It Yourself) store in Limerick, a small pottery in east Cork, a housewares chain store in Belgium and a supermarket in the south of France. Buying these things in countries on the continent isn't really as glamorous as it may seem; from this part of the world, it amounts to little more than traveling from state to state in the U.S. Carrying them back, however, is not as easy. But carry them we do – or rather my long suffering, though amazingly tolerant, husband does because the one time we had dishes shipped from Italy the hand-painted chickens we had chosen turned up as hand-painted fish, tigers and elephants! In our travels I also have acquired quite a few Portuguese green cabbage leaf plates and bowls and use them more than anything else because they go with everything (and, oddly, none of them were actually found in Portugal). The only time we were in that country, I never saw a single one in any shop I visited.

Table garden with cornflowers, snapdragons and verbena

Many of my settings involve making what I call "table gardens." Some of these I do by filling containers with bedding plants wedged closely together, and then adding individual flowers where necessary. When we wanted to celebrate our twentieth wedding anniversary in a big way, 120 friends and family were invited from the States as well as from here, the Continent and England, and we decided to have the party at the famed old Roof Garden in London. Situated on the top of an eight-story building above a department store in Kensington, its spacious rooms for dinner and dancing are surrounded by three mature gardens, complete with trees and ponds and even tame flamingos. Given that setting, I made a "garden" in a basket for each table with the hope that some guests would take them home and plant the contents. One lovely friend, Evie Karloff (Mrs. Boris), not only planted them, she pressed some of the flowers and sent them to us on a thank-you card to add to the memories of the night.

When using a basket, a plastic bowl or tub can be fitted inside (cutting the rim off if necessary), or the basket can be lined with strong plastic fixed on with hot glue. I have saved some of the wooden punnets that berries used to come in, as well as the cartons used by some cheesemakers, and the wood trays in which fruit from Italy is delivered to the grocers. In antique or junk shops, I keep my eye open for

Table garden with poppies

tin or enameled basins and other potential receptacles such as boxes with missing lids, or patterned and solid-colored bowls that are cracked or discolored on the inside where it won't show if they are full of growing things. I also have found that people greatly appreciate presents of plants arranged in baskets, garden trugs, earthenware casseroles, or other useful containers.

Rather than sticking the stems of random flowers right into the soil, I have found it is better to put them in something that holds water. I save a few plastic film containers and their lids to use in large arrangements, and I also have small, narrow prescription bottles which the pharmacist in our village ordered for me. A hole can be poked in the lids to stick the stem through and hold the flowers upright. The most useful containers of all are some small plastic bud vases a florist friend gave me. They can easily be pushed into the soil, but have very pointy ends, so if I am using something lined with plastic, I cut a piece of cork tile to fit the bottom of the container and put it in before adding the plants.

Many kinds of moss grow on the stone walls as well as in the woods, so I am always able to gather it as I need it, and when our flowers are flourishing, I make a different kind of table garden by placing a variety or sometimes just one kind of flower, such as poppies or snapdragons, upright into a platter, a shallow plastic-lined basket, or a tray filled with a layer of soaked oasis and covered with moss. Sometimes to give the effect that the garden is actually growing on the table, I use moss to cover any parts of the container that show – making sure that any moss that is touching the table is dry so it won't mark the wood or cloth. Wildflowers and grasses also make lovely gardens.

As Easter centerpieces for many years, instead of relying on moss to fill in the gaps, I have been growing grass seed in containers – sowing it well ahead of time and "mowing" it with scissors if it gets too long – and then sticking in miniature daffodils and small hyacinth, crocus or tulips, and scattering colored eggs among them.

Unexpectedly, the eggs at first presented a problem – there don't seem to be any white chicken eggs in Ireland, but quite by chance I discovered some pale beige duck eggs in our local grocery shop and the problem was solved.

To use up the eggs we always have Delia's Egg and Onion Dish for an after-Easter lunch.

Table garden with dried grasses

Egg and Onion Dish

1 hard-boiled egg and 1 onion per person
chicken stock
béchamel sauce made with milk, or milk and chicken stock
grated mild cheese

Slice the onions and boil them in the stock for five minutes. Slice the hard-boiled eggs. Arrange eggs and onions alternately in a buttered shallow baking dish, pour on the béchamel, sprinkle with some grated cheese and bake at 350° for 15 minutes.

Other than "table gardens," some of my favorite settings using flowers include integrating them with vegetables. Because the artichokes usually come in at the same time as many of the roses, I like combining them for a centerpiece. Besides, I just like the sound of the words "artichokes and roses." Sunflowers and round green squashes work well together as do yellow squash, tomatoes and various herb flowers. Actually, in order for the herbs to have full flavor, they shouldn't be allowed to flower at all, but I like to use the blossoms for garnishing, as well as in arrangements, so I always let some go. I am careful to use only edible flowers as garnishes and am particularly fond of those from basil, coriander, oregano, scented geranium, lavender, nasturtium violas, and the petals of pot marigold. Some varieties of beans bear beautiful scarlet flowers, but I don't use them profusely because for each one I pluck, we will have one less bean. Chive blossoms, when pulled apart, separate into lovely little bell shapes, and borage, which reseeds itself every year, has a flower with a slightly prickly dark base, which I remove and am left with a beautiful blue star. I often use dill flowers, both on their own and

Silver tankard
centerpieces

in mixed bouquets. Not only do they make a wonderful display, but they also fill the room with a delicious aroma. Dick De Neut (of the "berry sandwich") says that now, whenever he cooks with dill, he is reminded of our Irish cottage and wants to return for a "dill fix."

Richard gave me seven antique wooden ("treen") vessels that were originally for wine tasting. Their patina is so nice that it seems risky to put water in them, but since their initial purpose certainly forced them to contain something wet, I decided it should be safe to put flowers in them. In this case, I realized the goblets would hold water a lot longer than they did wine, so I only use them for a centerpiece, and – just to be safe – empty them as soon as possible.

Among the silver I inherited are some tankards which – like the treen goblets, with a single variety of flower bunched in each one – look beautiful, clustered in the middle of the table. Containers for bunches of flowers certainly don't have to be antiques or expensive; different-sized glassware, jugs, small baskets or bottles can be just as effective. We received a wedding present of Italian plates, hand-painted with a ribbon motif and, quite by chance, in Dublin I discovered some fabric printed in a similar design, and variations of that basic combination have become something I use over and over. Through the years I have acquired a fairly eclectic collection of table things, but by mixing, matching and looking out for something new (preferably a bargain, of course) to add in, unusual and pretty settings can be achieved with a lot less. The possibilities are endless.

Some menus and recipes for dinner parties :

LITTLE GEM CAESAR SALAD • CHICKEN IN RHUBARB SAUCE[*] • SAUTEED RUBY CHARD AND ONIONS[*] • BASMATI RICE • APPLE SPONGE PUDDING[*]

Little Gem is a very crisp, very short romaine type lettuce and is wonderful for Caesar Salad. My Caesar dressing is a sort of cheat because I use Thai fish sauce in place of anchovies.

Caesar Dressing

4 large garlic cloves, pressed or thoroughly mashed

4 teaspoons Thai fish sauce

2 teaspoons Dijon mustard

4 teaspoons red wine vinegar

$\frac{1}{2}$ cup olive oil

drops of hot pepper sauce

In a mini-processor, blend all the ingredients together.

Tab.

111

Chicken in Rhubarb Sauce

8–10 pieces crystallized ginger

4 garlic cloves

2 cups rhubarb jam

4 tablespoons cornstarch

4 tablespoons soy sauce

$\frac{1}{3}$ cup sherry

$\frac{1}{2}$ cup vinegar

3 cups chicken broth

6 chicken thighs, skinned

6 chicken breasts, skinned

1 cup toasted cashew pieces

Rinse ginger in hot water to remove the sugar, then chop it and the garlic and mix with the jam, cornstarch and the liquids. Pour into a heavy saucepan and simmer until thickened. Add the thighs, simmer them for 15 minutes and then put in the breasts, covering them well with the sauce, and simmer 20 minutes longer. Serve sprinkled with cashew nuts.

Serves 8–10.

This can be done well in advance and carefully reheated at serving time.

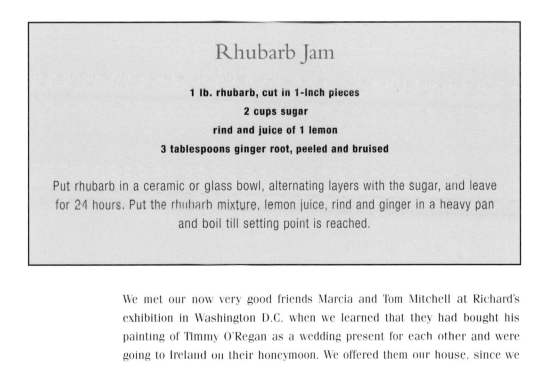

Rhubarb Jam

1 lb. rhubarb, cut in 1-inch pieces

2 cups sugar

rind and juice of 1 lemon

3 tablespoons ginger root, peeled and bruised

Put rhubarb in a ceramic or glass bowl, alternating layers with the sugar, and leave for 24 hours. Put the rhubarb mixture, lemon juice, rind and ginger in a heavy pan and boil till setting point is reached.

We met our now very good friends Marcia and Tom Mitchell at Richard's exhibition in Washington D.C. when we learned that they had bought his painting of Timmy O'Regan as a wedding present for each other and were going to Ireland on their honeymoon. We offered them our house, since we were going to be away at that time, and we thought they should meet Timmy.

Marcia left us a daily journal, ending each page with "Thank you for this day." Her account of their last day, unbeknownst to her, revealed a long standing fib of mine.

She wrote, "Picked rhubarb and made Tom a pie this morning." Because of my reluctance about making desserts, knowing nothing about rhubarb in general, and since he had no idea what it looked like, I had convinced Richard that our healthy plant had withered and died. I, of course, was shamed into admitting my ploy and now even have more than one plant. I actually have come to like the stuff myself when it isn't too sweet.

Sautéed Ruby Chard and Onions

$2^1/_2$ lbs. chard with its ribs
3 onions, chopped
2 tablespoons olive oil
3 tablespoons mayonnaise
salt and freshly ground pepper

Separate the chard leaves from their ribs and then wash them.
In a heavy saucepan cook the wet leaves with about $^1/_4$ cup more water, turning frequently for 4–6 minutes.
Rinse the leaves in cold water, drain, squeeze as dry as possible, and then roughly chop them. Cut the ribs into half-inch pieces, and steam them for about 10 minutes and set aside. In the heavy saucepan sauté the onions in the olive oil until translucent, add the chard ribs and then the chopped leaves. Cook, stirring, for about three minutes, and then stir in the mayonnaise and salt and pepper. Continue cooking, stirring until mayonnaise is thoroughly heated. Serves 8–10.

I grow mostly ruby chard because the color is so vibrant, and also because white chard ribs need to be blanched before further cooking so that they don't darken.

I cook beet greens the same way, using cooked diced beets along with the onions in the finished dish.

Apple Sponge Pudding

3 lbs. tart apples, peeled and thinly sliced

$^1/_2$ cup light brown sugar

juice and finely chopped rind of 2 lemons

6 oz. butter, softened

$^2/_3$ cup superfine sugar

2 eggs, beaten

2 cups self-rising flour

$^1/_2$ cup (or more) milk

Butter an 8-cup baking dish, put the apples in the bottom and sprinkle the light brown sugar and the lemon juice and rind over them. Beat the butter with the superfine sugar until fluffy, gradually beat in the eggs, and then lightly beat in the flour, adding as much milk as necessary to make a soft consistency that will easily drop from a spoon. Spread the mixture on the apples and bake at 350° for about 40 minutes until the sponge is set. Serve warm. Serves 8–10.

LOBSTER AND NECTARINES WITH WALNUT VINAIGRETTE* • LAMB STEW WITH FENNEL AND ARTICHOKES* • RICE AND ORZO PILAF* • SHREDDED YELLOW AND GREEN ZUCCHINI WITH DILL • HOMEMADE ICE CREAM

Lobster and Nectarines with Walnut Vinaigrette

3 1$^1/_2$-lb. lobsters, cooked and shelled

3 nectarines or peaches, blanched and peeled

chopped, deep-fried walnuts

Walnut Oil Vinaigrette

Slice lobster into 24 pieces. Slice the nectarines or peaches into 24 pieces. Arrange, alternating lobster and nectarines or peaches, on serving plates, sprinkling on some chopped fried walnuts and spooning over Walnut Oil Vinaigrette. Serves 6.

Lamb Stew with Fennel and Artichokes

4 lbs. lamb, cut in cubes

4 garlic cloves

juice of 1 lemon

1 bay leaf

lamb stock or chicken stock or both

fennel greens

8 fennel bulbs, cut in quarters and blanched for 5 minutes

6 cooked artichoke hearts, cut in quarters

chopped fennel fronds

M a r i n a d e :

a bottle of white wine

2 onions, chopped

2 carrots, chopped

a few lovage leaves or celery leaves

2 garlic cloves

2 tablespoons fennel seeds, crushed

1 teaspoon ground white pepper

$\frac{1}{2}$ cup olive oil

1 bay leaf

To make the marinade: In a processor combine the wine, onions, carrots, lovage or celery leaves, garlic, fennel seeds, pepper, and olive oil. Add the bay leaf and use the mixture to marinate the lamb cubes overnight.

Put the lamb, marinade, garlic cloves, lemon juice, and a fresh bay leaf in a casserole, and add enough stock to just cover. Lay the fennel greens on top, bring to a boil, cover, and bake at 350º for 45 minutes. Push aside the fennel greens, add the fennel bulbs, enough stock to cover again, replace the fennel greens, and bake, covered, 45 minutes more or until lamb is tender. Remove the fennel bulbs and lamb from the liquid (discard the greens and bay leaves), degrease the liquid and puree the bulbs with enough of the liquid, including garlic and any bits of vegetable to make a sauce. Add the artichoke hearts to the lamb and pour on the sauce. Reheat, and then put the stew on a serving platter.
Sprinkle with chopped fennel fronds. Serves 12.
Cream or yogurt can be added to the sauce.
Chunks of cooked lamb sausage make a nice addition to the stew, and if I want to stretch the servings I sometimes add a can of flageolet or haricot beans.

Rice and Orzo Pilaf

2 oz. butter

2 garlic cloves, chopped

1/2 cup chopped onions or shallots

1/3 cup orzo pasta

1 cup uncooked rice

2 cups chicken broth

a little lemon juice

freshly ground white pepper

In a heavy saucepan with a tight-fitting lid, melt the butter and gently sauté the garlic and onions for a few minutes. Add the noodles and rice and stir around a bit. Bring the chicken broth to a boil, pour it into the rice mixture, stir, and put on the lid. Simmer for 35 minutes and then let stand without opening for at least 10 minutes. Before serving, add a little lemon juice and some freshly ground white pepper. Serves 6.

ROASTED EGGPLANT SOUP* • CHICKEN WITH PRESERVED LEMONS AND OLIVES* • WHOLE WHEAT COUSCOUS • BUTTERED RUNNER BEANS WITH SUMMER SAVORY • MIXED GREEN SALAD • PEAR AND NECTARINE PUDDING*

In our part of Ireland, summer savory is a most reluctant herb, but when it does decide to grow, we have it for the whole season and I use it often, especially with all sorts of beans.

Roasted Eggplant Soup

3 eggplants

olive oil

8 garlic cloves

2 red peppers

1 large onion, chopped

a little Worcestershire sauce

about 3 pints chicken stock

salt and pepper

fresh chopped basil

Cut the eggplants in half, rub the cut sides with a little olive oil, and roast them at 400° for about 45 minutes. They should be somewhat browned. Roast the garlic, rubbed with a little olive oil, wrapped in foil, along with the eggplants. If there are any really tough bits of skin on the edges of the eggplants, trim them off and then puree them with their remaining skin and the garlic. Roast the peppers until the skins blister, and put them into a paper bag for about 10 minutes. Remove the skins and seeds, and puree.

Sauté the onion in a small amount of oil until just softened; add the eggplant puree, a bit of Worcestershire sauce and enough of the stock to make the soup a medium thick consistency. Simmer for 20 minutes and add salt and pepper if necessary. If the eggplants have been pureed in a blender, there probably won't be any visible skin, but if there is, sieve the soup before serving. To serve top each bowl with a swirl of pepper puree and a sprinkling of chopped basil. Serves 6–8.

I have been intrigued by the Moroccan use of preserved lemons, and have read many recipes containing them as well as many differing methods of preserving them. I've tried it several ways, including what seems to be the most traditional one which involves slicing the lemon vertically in quarters, leaving them attached at the bottom, and then packing them full of salt before putting them in a very strong brine. Another method is to slice the lemons and salt them overnight and then put them in oil. Yet another uses vinegar and brine.

I've also tried slicing them and putting them in an extra strong brine for which the instructions said it didn't matter if some of the salt didn't dissolve. About three inches of salt didn't dissolve and I decided it did matter and abandoned that effort.

Finally, I have been pleased with the results of combining several methods and had the inspiration that since the old brine is just outside the door, why not use sea water, boiled and cooled? We recently went to a Moroccan restaurant and tried some of their lemon and thought mine compared quite well. They used only the skin in quite large pieces, but I like to use both the skin and the pulp, finely chopped, or whirled in a processor, and I am finding it a wonderful addition to lots of different things.

**Centerpiece using
treen goblets**

Chicken with Preserved Lemons and Olives

4 chicken breasts and 4 thighs, skinned and boned

olive oil

1 teaspoon each, ground ginger, nutmeg, cumin and cinnamon

$^3/_4$ teaspoon paprika

white pepper

1$^1/_2$ cups chopped onion

4 garlic cloves, chopped

1 tablespoon grated fresh ginger

1 tablespoon lemon juice

chicken stock

6 slices preserved lemon, finely chopped

potato starch mixed with water

cracked green olives

Cut the chicken breasts into pieces about the same size as the thighs; rub them all with a little olive oil; sprinkle on a mixture of the ground ginger, nutmeg, cumin, cinnamon and paprika, and brown them in a nonstick pan. Grind some white pepper on the chicken pieces, put them aside, and in a heavy casserole, in a little olive oil sauté the onions, garlic and grated ginger until just soft, then stir in any of the remaining spice mixture, and the lemon juice. Put the chicken thighs on top, and add enough chicken stock to just barely cover. Simmer, covered, for 10 minutes, and then add the breasts and more stock to cover again and simmer, covered, for about 10 minutes more. Remove all the chicken to a serving platter and keep warm. Stir the chopped lemon into the casserole, bring to a simmer, and whisk in some potato starch mixture to thicken the sauce. Serve on a platter surrounded by couscous and topped with the sauce and pieces of cracked (pitted) green olives. Serves 6.

Preserved Lemons

8 lemons, sliced and pitted

kosher salt

sea water or a 10 percent brine

white vinegar

Put the lemons in a colander, sprinkle them generously with kosher salt, and leave them to drain for 24 hours. Put them in a jar, cover them with a solution made of equal portions of sea water/brine and vinegar, and leave them to cure at room temperature for two weeks. Rinse them before using. (Refrigerate after the initial two-week curing.).

Lamb is just as good used with the preserved lemon recipe.

Pear and Nectarine Pudding

2 tablespoons sugar combined with 2 teaspoons flour

2 cups crème fraiche

2 eggs, beaten

2 teaspoons vanilla

3 pears and 3 nectarines, peeled and quartered

superfine sugar

Mix the sugar and flour mixture into a little of the crème fraiche until well combined, add eggs and vanilla, and then whisk the mixture into the remaining crème fraiche. Arrange the pears and nectarines in a baking dish, pour over the crème fraiche mixture, and bake at 350º for 30 minutes. Cool (or refrigerate). Sprinkle some superfine sugar over the top and stick the dish under a hot broiler for about five minutes to caramelize. Watch carefully. Serves 6–8.

Crème Fraiche

1 pint whipping cream   **1 tablespoon buttermilk**

Combine cream and buttermilk and heat slowly to 75º–85º (no more). Pour the cream into a bowl, cover, and keep at about 75º for 8–24 hours.

CELERY ROOT SALAD WITH TOASTED PECANS[*] • COD BAKED IN SPANISH CHORIZO SAUCE[*] • SAUTEED CABBAGE WITH TARRAGON • SAUTEED CHERRY TOMATOES • LONG GRAIN AND WILD RICE • RHUBARB AND OATMEAL CRUMBLE[*]

Celery Root Salad

1 large knob of celery root   **Egg White/walnut oil Mayonnaise**

2 fennel bulbs   **mixed lettuces**

4 medium Jerusalem artichokes   **Walnut Oil Vinaigrette**

2 pears   **toasted pecan pieces**

Microwave celery root 6 minutes (or boil whole 20–30 minutes). Blanch fennel 1–2 minutes. Peel and slice the celery root, fennel, Jerusalem artichokes and pears into matchstick pieces and coat them all with the mayonnaise. To serve, mound in center of plates and surround with mixed greens lightly dressed with Walnut Oil Vinaigrette. Sprinkle pecan pieces over top. Serves 8.

Egg White Mayonnaise

2 egg whites
1 teaspoon Dijon mustard
2 tablespoons white wine vinegar
salt
$\frac{1}{2}$ cup vegetable oil or walnut oil

Mix whites, mustard, vinegar and salt in processor.
Gradually pour on oil until emulsified.

Cod Baked in Spanish Chorizo Sauce

1 cup white wine
2 cups chicken stock
6 garlic cloves, crushed
1 cup cream
8 oz. chorizo sausage, sliced
8 pieces thick cod fillet, skinned, weighing 6 oz. each
potato flour mixed with a little water
chopped parsley or other herbs

Boil together the wine, stock and garlic for a few minutes, add the cream and the chorizo, and simmer for 20 minutes. Remove and discard the chorizo. Put the cod in a baking dish, pour on the hot liquid, and bake at 425° for 10–15 minutes. Carefully remove the cod to a warm serving plate and cover it with foil. Strain the cooking liquid into a heavy saucepan, bring it to a simmer and whisk in some potato starch mixture to thicken. Pour some sauce over the fish, sprinkle on some chopped herbs, and serve the rest of the sauce on the side. Serves 8.

I am able to buy two kinds of chorizo in Cork, one of which has anise added. They both are spicy, but not overly hot, and add a wonderful flavor to the sauce. If I am using the one with anise, I put a little Pernod in the cooking liquid.

Rhubarb and Oatmeal Crumble

$1^1/_2$ cups plain flour

$1^1/_2$ cups oatmeal

1 cup brown sugar, lightly packed

1 teaspoon ground cinnamon

6 oz. softened butter

2 cups stewed rhubarb

$^1/_2$ cup lightly toasted pistachios, chopped

Combine the flour, oatmeal, brown sugar and cinnamon in a deep bowl. Drop in the butter in pieces and rub them in with your hands until the mixture looks like coarse bread crumbs. Press half of the mixture into a rectangular ceramic or glass baking dish, spread on the rhubarb, top with the rest of the oatmeal mixture, sprinkle on the nuts, and bake at 375° for 35 minutes. Serves 8.
Serve warm or cool with cream, crème fraiche, or vanilla ice cream.

SHRIMP BAKED WITH TOMATOES AND GOAT CHEESE[*] • CHICKEN WITH LEMON ZEST AND FENNEL[*] • SAUTEED BEET GREENS AND CHOPPED PINK AND WHITE BEETS • NEW POTATOES WITH MINT • BIBB AND LITTLE GEM LETTUCE SALAD • BREAD PUDDING WITH BLACK CHERRIES

Shrimp Baked with Tomatoes and Goat Cheese

1 lb. shrimp, cooked in sea water and shelled

$1^1/_2$ lbs. peeled, chopped and deseeded tomatoes

2 garlic cloves pureed with a little salt

freshly ground white pepper

$1^1/_2$ tablespoons lemon thyme leaves

2 shallots, chopped

1 tablespoon olive oil

8 oz. goat cheese

Mix the shrimp with the tomatoes and garlic, add a little pepper and one tablespoon of lemon thyme, and let it marinate a few hours or overnight. Sauté the shallots in the olive oil for a few minutes, and stir in the tomatoes and shrimp. Divide the mixture between six scallop shells, put a round of goat cheese on top, and bake at 425° for 10 minutes. Just before serving sprinkle a little lemon thyme on top. Serves 4–6.

Chicken with Lemon Zest and Fennel

zest of 4 small lemons, very finely chopped	2 chicken breasts,
5 garlic cloves, chopped	weighing about 2 lbs. with bone
1 tablespoon whole fennel seed, ground	lemon juice
$1^1/_2$ cups parsley leaves	3 fennel heads, cut in half, blanched and
1/4 cup fresh tarragon leaves	rubbed with olive oil
salt and freshly ground pepper	3 onions, cut in quarters
olive oil	chicken broth mixed with lemon juice
	large green olives, pitted

In a processor mix together the lemon zest, garlic, ground fennel, parsley, tarragon, and a bit of salt and pepper, then add enough olive oil to make a paste. Stuff the paste under the chicken skin, and rub the chicken all over with a little olive oil and lemon juice. Put it in a baking dish, surround with the fennel and onions, and roast at 400°, basting the chicken and vegetables with the chicken broth and lemon juice, for 45–60 minutes. Before serving, scatter pitted green olives around the dish. Serves 4–6.

Be sure the lemon zest is just the yellow part. When I got careless and left on too much of the white part, the dish turned out to be quite bitter. When carving the chicken, I often remove the skin. The paste will stay stuck to the chicken slices.

SPAGHETTI LIMONE* • ORANGE ROASTED DUCK* • HUNGARIAN CABBAGE* • ROASTED RATTE POTATOES • MIXED SALAD WITH SPINACH AND WATERCRESS • SHERRY TRIFLE*

Spaghetti Limone

rind of 1 lemon, grated	olive oil
1 cup heavy cream	juice of 2 lemons
1 tablespoon grappa (or vodka)	salt and pepper
8 oz. spaghetti	

Steep the lemon rind in the cream over very low heat for 20 minutes. Stir in grappa and bring just to a boil. Remove from heat, cover, and leave as long as you like. Cook the spaghetti in water, a drop of olive oil and juice of one lemon. Drain, put in a heavy saucepan, and toss with the rest of the lemon juice. Reheat the cream mixture, pour it over the spaghetti, add salt and pepper, and stir/toss over low heat until the spaghetti has absorbed some of the sauce. Serves 4–6 as a first course.

Orange Roasted Duck

2 or more fresh ducks
1 or more oranges
2 garlic cloves per duck
orange juice

Carefully prick skin of each duck all over without piercing the flesh. Put half an orange and
two cloves of smashed garlic inside each duck, set ducks on racks in roasting pans and
roast them at 400° for one hour, removing rendered fat often or the oven may catch fire.
Turn oven down to 325°, and roast one hour more. Finally, continue to roast, basting with
orange juice every 10 minutes for a final hour (or better, inject with a culinary syringe).
Remove the skin and take the meat off in strips. Serve with Coriander Chutney.
*The ducks will be very tender and moist, and can be held up to two days well wrapped, on or
off the bone. I serve only the legs with the skin on – they can be crisped in the oven.
I allow one duck for two or possibly three people.*

Sherry Trifle is the one dessert I make most often. It is another of my favorite
cheats, because I have found that Jello instant vanilla pudding tastes just as
good as custard sauce. It is not available in Ireland and I don't like the English
custard powder as much, so I always get some from the States.

Sherry Trifle

an 8-inch sponge cake, split in half crosswise
strawberry jam
medium dry sherry
canned peach and pear quarters in water
6 cups Jello vanilla instant pudding
whipped cream
toasted, slivered almonds

In an 8-inch glass bowl with straight sides, put one round piece of sponge cake,
spread it with strawberry jam, generously sprinkle with sherry, put enough fruit slices on
top to cover, and spread on half of the pudding. Repeat the layer, pipe on some
whipped cream and sprinkle with the almonds. Serves 6–8.
*This might not serve as many people if Twiggy or my Aunt Dellie happened to be a guest.
They both, on different occasions, took very small portions, and then
just kept going back for more.*

TERRINE OF TWO SALMONS, CRAB AND WATERCRESS* • WHITE
VEAL STEW WITH FLAGEOLET BEANS* • SUGAR SNAP PEAS
WITH OLIVE OIL AND LEMON ZEST • BUTTERED NOODLES •
MIXED GREEN AND HERB SALAD • SUMMER PUDDING*

123

Terrine of Two Salmons, Crab and Watercress

12 oz. boneless, skinned salmon	4 oz. cream cheese
3 tablespoons lemon juice	12 oz. fresh crab meat
2 tablespoons dry vermouth	4 cups watercress leaves
2 tablespoons minced shallots	2 tablespoons good mayonnaise
2 teaspoons light vegetable oil	2 tablespoons heavy cream
1 teaspoon salt	a 6 oz. piece of smoked salmon
$^1/_2$ teaspoon freshly ground white pepper	1 cup chopped watercress
10 large dark green lettuce or beet leaves,	$^1/_2$ cup plain yogurt
blanched, with center ribs removed	$^1/_2$ cup mayonnaise

Roughly cut up the fresh salmon and let it marinate for an hour in a combination
of the lemon juice, vermouth, shallots, oil, salt and pepper.
Line an oiled 10 x 3 x 2–inch terrine with the lettuce leaves, leaving some
hanging over the edge. Puree the salmon and its marinade with the cream cheese,
stir in the crab meat, and spread half of the mixture on top of lettuce or beet leaves.
Finely chop the watercress, mix it with the mayonnaise and cream and spread half of it on
top of the salmon mixture. Cut the smoked salmon into very small cubes and put them on
top of watercress. Spread on the remaining watercress mixture, top with the
remaining salmon, and fold on the overhanging lettuce or beet leaves.
Put the terrine, covered, in a roasting pan with enough hot water to come halfway up
its sides, and bake at 350° for one hour. Cool, weight down, and chill overnight, draining
any liquid that collects. Unmold and cut into fairly thick slices. Serve with a sauce of
chopped watercress stirred into a combination of yogurt and mayonnaise. Serves 6–8.

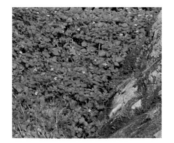

White Veal Stew with Flageolet Beans

2$\frac{1}{2}$ lbs. veal stew meat

olive oil

chicken stock

rosemary tied in a muslin bag

20 pearl onions, blanched and peeled

20 small mushrooms, halved

2 tablespoons chopped rosemary, plus a little more for garnish

potato starch mixed with water

cream or crème fraiche

salt and freshly ground white pepper

2 cups cooked flageolet beans

In a nonstick pan, lightly brown the veal cubes in a little olive oil, transfer them to a heavy casserole, pour on the stock, add the rosemary tied in muslin, and simmer for about 1$\frac{1}{4}$ hours. Take the veal pieces out of the stock and set aside, keeping them warm. Discard the rosemary. Lightly sauté the onions and mushrooms separately. Bring the stock to a boil, stir in the chopped rosemary, and simmer for five minutes. Add the onions and simmer five minutes more, then add the mushrooms and simmer three minutes. Then, still simmering, whisk in the potato starch mixture, a little cream or crème fraiche, salt if necessary, and white pepper. Stir in the veal and flageolet beans. Gently reheat before transferring the stew to a warm serving dish. Sprinkle on a bit more chopped rosemary. Serves 6–8.

GRAVLAX TARTARE* • LEG OF LAMB IN HAY* • CARROTS WITH HORSERADISH SAUCE* • GRILLED ZUCCHINI WITH CHOPPED HERBS • COLCANNON • BAKED ORANGES*

Gravlax Tartare

a piece of gravlax weighing 2–3 lbs.

2 cups finely chopped dill

gravlax sauce

salmon caviar

Cut gravlax away from skin and chop it finely. Don't use a processor or meat grinder – the fish will get too mushy. Form the chopped gravlax into round cakes, about 3 oz. each, and roll their sides in chopped dill. Serve topped with a spoonful of the gravlax sauce and some salmon caviar. Spoon some more sauce around the cakes. Serves at least 8–10.

Gravlax

3 lbs. middle section of salmon with skin

1 large bunch of dill, chopped

$1/4$ cup kosher salt

$1/4$ cup sugar

2 tablespoons coarsely ground white pepper

2 tablespoons gin

Split the salmon and remove all bones. Leave skin on. Mix the dill, salt, sugar and pepper. Put one piece of the salmon skin-side down in a nonmetal casserole and spread with the dill mixture. Sprinkle on the gin and put the other piece of fish on top. Cover with plastic wrap and weight down. Leave in fridge for at least three days, turning and basting with the juices daily.

Gravlax Sauce

4 tablespoons dark, strong mustard

3 tablespoons brown sugar

2 tablespoons white wine vinegar

1 tablespoon dry mustard

3 tablespoons chopped fresh dill

$1/3$ cup olive oil

Mix all the ingredients except oil in a processor, and then slowly add the oil as if for mayonnaise.

Carrots with Horseradish Sauce

8 medium carrots, coarsely chopped
5 tablespoons mayonnaise
2 tablespoons prepared horseradish

Steam or microwave carrots until cooked but not too soft.
Mix them with the mayonnaise and horseradish, and serve hot.
*This is enough for eight large spoonfuls, but I usually increase or even double the quantity
because it is always very popular, and is just as good cold or warmed up if there is any left
over. It is also good served in a shallow baking dish with bread crumbs on top and
lightly browned under the broiler.*

Centerpiece with sunflowers and dahlias, surrounded with crab claws and dill sauce

Baked Oranges

5 small oranges

2 cups water

2 cups sugar

2 tablespoons Cointreau

orange zest, blanched and cut into thin strips

cream cheese

chopped, toasted hazelnuts

In a saucepan cover the oranges with water and boil them for 15 minutes. Pour this water away and cover them again, bring to a boil, remove the oranges, cut them into quarters, and put them in a baking dish. Make a syrup with the water and sugar, pour it over the oranges, and bake at 350° for 30 minutes. Cool and refrigerate the oranges in the syrup with Cointreau added. Serve at room temperature with orange zest on top. Makes at least 8–10 servings.

Form the cream cheese into walnut-sized balls and roll them in the hazelnuts. Serve a plate of cheese balls along with the oranges.

The oranges will keep in the fridge for a long time.

Ava with her father in Ireland
(Facing) Michael and Pat York
in Ava's front garden

Richard McKenzie

Favorite Times

From the
left:
Richard,
Maureen
O'Hara,
Robert
Osborne and
Jane Powell

CHAPTER EIGHT

"They Can't Take That Away From Me"

People & Places

Although Thanksgiving isn't a holiday in Ireland, it is one of my most favorite times and so deeply ingrained in our heritage that we've never known Americans living abroad who don't celebrate it. Because we treat the day with such tradition, I suppose it is understandable that some people here confuse it with other American holidays. Once a dinner guest said, "This is your Fourth of July, isn't it?" Richard agreed that our summers might sometimes seem that way, but even in Ireland, July is not in November.

Some years back, fresh turkeys were not easy to come by at any time other than Christmas. We thought we had the problem solved because Kitty O'Regan was raising some and offered us one, which she would also clean so it would be ready for the oven. Explaining our American holiday to her, we asked if she minded if we had it in November instead. A couple of weeks later, I was having a cup of tea with Kitty in her kitchen, when a turkey came gobbling to the door looking for a handout. She proudly informed me that this was her best turkey and it was designated for us. I hope I seemed suitably impressed, because I couldn't have told her that there was no way I could cook a bird I had personally met. When the time came, we assured Kitty it was perfect and thanked her, but we gave it to the police sergeant.

Our next Thanksgiving here we got wrong ourselves by never having realized that the celebration is not on the last Thursday in November, but the fourth one, and it wasn't until someone phoned from the States to ask if we'd had a nice holiday that we discovered we had missed it.

Another time, when Kitty was no longer raising turkeys (thank goodness), I ordered one from a farmer we didn't know so there was no danger of meeting the doomed bird. The turkey arrived cleaned, but as I was stuffing only the cavity, I didn't realize until it came out of the oven that the neck end was full of grain. I disposed of it and no one was the wiser, but it had a nice toasted aroma and I have often wondered if maybe we missed an interesting new taste experience.

Fresh (and even better, free-range) turkeys are now available at all times of the year, but – as we found out just before our most recent Thanksgiving – that doesn't mean that acquiring one might not be eventful. The small supermarket in a nearby town supplies lots of turkeys, and their specialty is boning, stuffing and rolling them. As we were going to be away until just before Thanksgiving, I ordered a bird in early November and, to be safe, specified that it not be boned and rolled. On the Tuesday I phoned to ask if I could collect my turkey the next day, and to remind them about the boning and rolling. They were adamant that they knew all about our American Thanksgiving and I was not to worry. We went to get it on Wednesday afternoon and there it was – the only turkey in the shop – boned and rolled. Of course the person on duty was not the one who knew all about Thanksgiving, but someone who couldn't understand why I didn't want it boned and rolled since he was sure that was the way the order had been placed. Keeping calm, I asked him to please check the order book. He disappeared into the office and returned with an ancient, enormous red book which, when opened, we discovered was missing a page – the page containing my order. Not to worry, he said, he would telephone the farmer who would catch a new turkey, prepare it and deliver it to our village that evening before the shops there closed. I don't suppose at this point it is even necessary to say that when we went into the village at the appointed time there was no turkey. More phone calls, more not-to-worrys, it would be delivered early the next morning. LATE the next morning it was, barely in time to get it in the oven, but we did, and I had an added reason for giving thanks.

A method of rescuing an overcooked turkey came out of a Thanksgiving we had while my father was making a film in Ireland. Daddy requested that we be with him as much as possible, which meant that we lived and ate in various remote accommodations because they were filming all around the country. The only other American in the international film company was a very homesick young Edward Albert. I had promised Edward a home-cooked traditional Thanksgiving dinner if the location shoot was reasonably near our house at the time. As it happened, we were only an hour's drive away, so Richard went home to work and I joined him a few days before the holiday to get ready. Edward, in turn, invited the Italian ingenue and her French interpreter who wanted to experience something so uniquely American.

I was actually able to find cranberries, sweet potatoes, ingredients for pumpkin pies (not easy in those days – in fact, one of the camera crew arranged for a pumpkin to be sent down on the train by someone who grew them near Dublin), and had located a good-sized turkey. Preparations went without incident until a very disappointed Edward rang early on the day to say the location had been moved. The scene required a storm on a beach, and the director had heard one was due at another beach further away. They couldn't come after all. I assured him we could do it another day, and turned off the oven. Some time later,

A method of rescuing an overcooked turkey came out of a Thanksgiving we had while my father was making a film in Ireland.

Edward phoned again to say they were on their way after all, because the storm had become too fierce to shoot, and asked if they could bring a few other members of the crew. I put the turkey in the oven. When his next frantic call said they were lost, I directed them back on course and turned down the oven. He had said he was desperately looking forward to the nostalgic smell of roasting turkey, so I was determined to keep it going until they turned up. By the time they should have arrived, Edward rang to say they had stopped at a pub. When they finally appeared, in full holiday spirit, they were, indeed, met by the turkey aroma, but I was pretty sure the bird itself would be a disaster. However, unchagrined, and happy to at last be in the middle of the Thanksgiving cooking, Mr. Albert said he could rescue the turkey – if I had an injector syringe. I did. He kept on roasting, and every few minutes basted and then injected a mixture of orange juice, honey and stock. The turkey was truly saved (it was still good when Daddy came for leftovers the next day). The holiday meal was a great success. The French and Italian initiates loved our standard Thanksgiving fare and even asked for recipes, especially the cranberry relish which they found most unusual, as well as an Indian dish that we have been including for years. One Sunday lunch in London, along with the roast lamb, Lynda gave us stir-fried cabbage that she had adapted from an Indian recipe. We liked it so much that shortly after, when she came to us for Thanksgiving, we asked her to do it again, and now it has become a tradition.

Cranberry, Orange, Apple and Onion Relish

2 cups cranberries
1 large unpeeled orange, cut in segments and seeded
2 tart apples, cored and quartered
$^1/_2$ cup sugar
1 medium mild onion, finely chopped
2 tablespoons rinsed and finely chopped crystallized ginger

In a processor grind together the cranberries, the orange, the apples and the sugar. Stir in the onion and the ginger and let the mixture sit for at least one day. Makes about 4 cups.

Lynda's Indian Cabbage

4–6 tablespoons vegetable oil
1 tablespoon whole cumin seeds
1 large Savoy cabbage, shredded
1 lb. carrots, grated
$^1/_4$ teaspoon ground turmeric
$^1/_4$ teaspoon ground cayenne

$^1/_2$ teaspoon salt
$^1/_2$ teaspoon sugar
$^1/_2$ teaspoon ground cardamom
$^1/_2$ teaspoon ground cumin
$^1/_2$ cup chopped cilantro (fresh coriander)

Heat the oil in a wok, add the cumin seeds, stir them around for a few seconds and then add the cabbage and carrots, stirring for about a minute. Add the turmeric and cayenne, stir, cover and cook over low heat for about five minutes. Stir in salt and sugar, and cook, covered, a few minutes more. Then stir in the cardamom, the cumin, and finally the chopped cilantro. Serves 8.

Situated as we are, five miles from the nearest village and at the end of a boreen, we've had pretty surprising drop-ins as well as planned guests at this little farmhouse over the years. Among those unexpectedly encountered at our front gate were Hurd Hatfield (the first actor to play Dorian Gray in a movie), who Aunt Dellie sent to us before we met again at Lismore, and Angela Lansbury and Peter Shaw who we, in turn, had taken to meet Aunt Dellie. Columnist Rex Reed continued along to us on his first visit to the country after he found that Angela wasn't home – ninety miles away. A Bavarian baroness (also sent by Aunt Dellie) appeared one Sunday morning as we were having breakfast, and fourteen of our son Tyler's Austrian schoolmates (whom he forgot to mention he had invited to stay for a week) arrived when Ty was away at a summer job. Juliet Prowse came for a few days, never once put on any makeup and, with the famous legs hidden in coveralls and wellies, experienced digging her first potatoes and gathering mussels. Like so many others, Juliet and her companion mistook the bright evening light for late afternoon, and when they arrived back from their drive they were mortified to learn it was nearly 10:00 p.m. Dinner (chicken, rather than lamb in hay) however, was not ruined.

It is so peaceful and quiet here that most of our friends who come to stay really can relax in a way they are unable to in other places, and despite protests that they are very early risers, find themselves sleeping at least until 10 o'clock if not until noon! Our very dear friend Brother Angelo, a Franciscan friar, visits nearly every summer, and in spite of his traditional brown habit, Angelo is a colorful figure in the garden or walking in the village. The good friar also has a wicked sense of humor, and his arrival is always eagerly anticipated by our local friends as well. Especially the equally wicked-humored sisters, Moira and Deirdre Collins, who insist on having him to supper at least once during his stay.

. . . most of our friends who come to stay really can relax in a way they are unable to in other places.

When we are having a few people at home for a dinner with Angelo I usually feature – what else, but - monkfish.

Monkfish with Cabbage and Mustard

3 lbs. monkfish tail, in one or several pieces

salt and pepper

2 tablespoons olive oil

2 heads of Savoy cabbage, shredded

6 slices Canadian bacon, chopped

4 large shallots, chopped

5 tablespoons chopped fresh tarragon

1$^1/_2$ cups hot fish stock

1 cup hot chicken stock

5 tablespoons Provencal or any nonsweet mustard

1 teaspoon English mustard

potato flour mixed with a little water

Brother Angelo in
the front garden

Trim all the grey membrane from the monkfish tail and pound it a bit to even out thickness. Salt and pepper it, quickly sear it in a little olive oil and set it aside. (If I have missed any of the membrane it will be visible after searing and I can then remove it). Blanch the cabbage for only a few seconds and then drain and rinse it in cold water. Lightly brown the bacon, add the shallots, sauté to soften, and mix with the cabbage and tarragon. Put half the cabbage mixture in a heavy casserole, place the monkfish on top and cover with remaining cabbage. Pour on hot stock. Roast, covered, at 425° for about 30 minutes, depending on thickness of fish. (It is a good idea to check for doneness after 20 minutes, and to continue checking every 5 minutes – it may take longer than 30 minutes, but not much.) Remove the fish, and cut it into serving-size pieces. Drain the cabbage, reserving all liquid, and put the fish and cabbage aside, covered with foil to keep them warm.

Boil the liquid until it is reduced by about half, reduce heat to medium, stir in the mustards, and then whisk in enough of the potato flour mixture to thicken the sauce.

Put the cabbage in a warmed serving dish, top with the fish and pour on the mustard sauce. Serves 8.

Monkfish with Zucchini

$1\frac{1}{2}$ lbs. monkfish

1 lb. yellow and green zucchini

salt and freshly ground white pepper

olive oil

$1\frac{1}{2}$ cups white wine or vermouth

2 tablespoons rosemary, chopped

1 large onion, sliced

a little potato starch mixed to a thin paste with water

Rouille

Cut the monkfish into $1\frac{1}{2}$-inch pieces, making sure that all of the grey membrane is removed. Cut the zucchini into $1\frac{1}{2}$- by $\frac{1}{2}$ inch pieces. Lightly salt and pepper the fish pieces, sauté them in a little olive oil just until they begin to lose their translucency, and remove them to a bowl. Stir the wine or vermouth into the pan, add the fish juices that have collected in the bowl, simmer for a few minutes, stir in the chopped rosemary, and put aside. (Degrease the liquid if necessary.) Sauté the onions for a few minutes in a little olive oil to soften, and add the zucchini, stirring for a minute or so. Then add the reserved liquid, simmer until the zucchini is lightly cooked, and add the fish pieces, simmering until they are just firm. Remove the fish and vegetables, boil the liquid to reduce a little, thicken with a little potato starch mixture, and then whisk in a few spoonfuls of rouille. To serve, pour the rouille sauce over the fish and vegetables, gently reheat and have a bowl of pure rouille on the side.

Rouille

$\frac{1}{3}$ cup basil leaves

8 garlic cloves, pureed with a little salt

$\frac{1}{3}$ cup drained canned pimientos

$\frac{1}{3}$ cup fresh bread crumbs

2 egg yolks

1 cup oil ($\frac{1}{3}$ olive oil and $\frac{2}{3}$ vegetable oil)

a little hot pepper sauce

Chop the basil in a processor; add the garlic, pimientos, bread crumbs and yolks, and process until well combined. With the motor running, slowly pour in the oil until the mixture is of a consistency like thin mayonnaise (it may not be necessary to use all the oil). Add a few drops of hot pepper sauce.

When the veteran Hollywood columnist Army
Archerd was doing a piece on Ireland, we
expected Army and his wife, Selma, to come
for lunch and asked them to collect Maureen
O'Hara and her daughter, Bronwyn, on the
way down. As I always do, I had checked with
them all to see if there was anything they
couldn't eat: no garlic for Army and Selma,
and no spinach for Maureen. I didn't tell them
I had planned spinach pasta with fresh
tomato, basil and garlic. But Maureen said
that she and Bronwyn love garlic. I decided
on two dishes, one with and one without, and
when Selma also happened to mention that
she loves crab, I phoned Cyril the postman.

Postman Cyril delivering crab claws

The day before, I went into the village to pick up some provisions and ran into
old friends, Michael and Pat York, looking for a cup of tea and a sandwich.
They had decided to do some last-minute sightseeing when Michael was given
a few days off from filming in Dublin. The Yorks knew we lived in Ireland, but
we hadn't seen each other in a long time and they didn't realize they had
stumbled upon our village. I insisted that they come home and have tea and
sandwiches with us, and judging from his expression, my husband, unusually
unkempt and taking out the rubbish, was hardly prepared to confront a film
star carrying my groceries through the garden gate. I also had nothing for
sandwiches but tomatoes, lettuce and spring onion. That combination,
however, is often on menus in Ireland, and is known simply as a "salad
sandwich." With the excellent brown bread and some good mayonnaise, it has
become one of our staples.

Lunch the next day got off to a shaky start. Having taken numerous wrong
turns, our guests were a couple of hours late; Army wasn't feeling very well,
but he is so nice that at first he didn't want to mention it and spoil the party;
Bronwyn reminded her mother that she is allergic to crab after Maureen had
already eaten some; and Selma was convinced that she was coming down with
pneumonia.

Bronwyn saved the day when she gave poor Army an over-the-counter-remedy
tablet she always carries for similar upsets. Bronwyn said she hadn't offered
them earlier because she somehow had the impression that Richard was a
doctor. Army's discomfort was soon alleviated, and although she was hesitant
to try any more, Maureen said it was the best crab she had ever tasted. When

we spoke later. I was assured she felt fine, thought her problems with crab might have been overcome at last, and we all agreed that Selma was probably just fatigued from all the traveling. You can't expect to get it right every time, but I was so relieved that what could have been the lunch party from hell ended on a very happy note.

A year or so later we had a call from columnist and Turner Classic Movies host Robert Osborne saying he was planning a visit to Ireland with Jane Powell and her husband, Dick Moore, and they hoped to see us. The Moores were going to stay with friends, and we pleaded with Bob to accept his long-standing invitation to stay at Clonlea. My head reeled. Although they are both our friends of many years, an Irish farmhouse does not figure in either Army's or Robert's normal territory. It was such an odd twist, I felt that since we'd had lunch for Mr. Archerd of *Daily Variety*, I had to repeat it for Mr. Osborne, his counterpart from the *Hollywood Reporter*, and Bob was thrilled at the idea of being with Maureen O'Hara on his first visit to Ireland. So I planned a lunch for ten.

It was early autumn and most of our garden had been ravaged by a Force-9 gale, but the wild heather had just come in, and I was able to fill my silver tankards and antique pitchers with a mixture of heather, rose hips and red berries as decorations down the center of a long table covered with a rust-colored cloth we usually use for Thanksgiving.

Even if Maureen had overcome her allergy, this time crab claws were definitely not an option (one of the guests was allergic to shellfish), so we started with summer squash and carrot soup. For the main course we had a salad that included chicken and bacon along with whatever I could salvage from the garden, and on the side, baked ratte potatoes with Greek yogurt and chives. Dessert was summer pudding and an apple crisp, followed by Gubbeen cheese.

Jane Powell starred in *Royal Wedding* with my father, but I hadn't seen her since I was nine years old, and we hadn't met her husband, Dick Moore, who must get so bored when people bring up the fact that he gave Shirley Temple her first screen kiss. My Richard didn't mention it but he was still envious. Maureen and Bronwyn were delayed again but this time because their nice friend Patrick, whom they had persuaded to be their driver and who was also joining us for lunch, had to help deliver a calf at the last minute, thereby requiring another shower. This time everyone was in good form with high spirits and reminiscences, and it turned into an old Hollywood "hooley" stretching into an early evening. We wished Army could have been there.

Fresh Tomato, Garlic and Basil Sauce

3 lbs. plum tomatoes, peeled and seeded

4 garlic cloves, finely chopped

2 garlic cloves mashed with a little salt

at least 2 cups roughly chopped basil leaves

$^1\!/_4$ cup best olive oil

Chop tomato into small cubes, making sure that all seeds are removed. (I am a fiend about this – it takes careful scrutiny, but I think it is worth the trouble.) Combine all ingredients and leave overnight or as long as possible to develop flavor. Serve at room temperature on hot fettuccini noodles.

Summer Squash and Carrot Soup

onion, chopped

4 pints chicken broth

2 lbs. mixed summer squash, chopped

1 lb. carrots, chopped

salt and freshly ground white pepper

nutmeg

cream

Cook the onion in a little chicken broth for about 5 minutes, and then add the squash, carrots and rest of the broth. Simmer for 30 minutes, puree in a blender, and add salt (if needed), pepper and a few grindings of nutmeg. Serve topped with a spoonful of lightly whipped cream. Serves 10.

Early Autumn Salad

a head of crisp lettuce, torn into small pieces

a chicken, roasted and cut into bite-size chunks

12 slices of Canadian bacon, cooked and cut into small pieces

3 medium beets (white, pink and golden), cooked and cubed

20 1$^1\!/_2$-inch yellow and green scallop squash, cooked and quartered

2 cups runner beans, cooked and thinly sliced

a handful of watercress

6 Jerusalem artichokes, cut in $^1\!/_2$-inch pieces

Shallot Vinaigrette

Toss all together and dress with Shallot Vinaigrette. Serves 10.

High among reassuring moments are those warm summer evenings when we can hear the children laughing and see them silhouetted in the late sunset as they fish from the rocks and swim off the jetty. We used to watch the O'Regan children gather there with other locals and several dogs, and now we often join them with their own children. It seems another world. My childhood was fairly sheltered and so vastly different, but such evenings always remind Richard of his early years by the sea, and after our sons had grown, returned to America and begun families of their own, I was pleased to realize that now my memories include so many Irish children, too, and that the young continue to be a cherished part of our life.

Nora O'Regan was a very little girl when we became neighbors. Initially only visiting with her dad, Timmy, Nora's uninhibited curiosity brought her venturing down the hill to us on her own and very soon she became my assistant around the place (my husband says "playmate"). She liked all the kitchen gadgets unknown to her but then she wanted no part of the "strange" things I prepared with them. Not even pasta. Although we hear she is still not adventuresome about food, these days Nora is often seen tearing along the road on her motorbike, a vibrant young woman, with those lovely eyes and shining smile nearly obliterated by her helmet, and I treasure the many times we romped together on the bales after haying and when I costumed her as Stan Laurel for the children's fancy-dress parade.

In his teens now, Matthew Neuberger often comes to join me in the kitchen during his holidays from London, and I'm still astounded at his remarkable memory when he was ten or eleven and wanted to make pickled shallots. Matthew wrote nothing down when we looked at the recipe and, though the process took several days, he never forgot a measurement or ingredient. Then there was Sean Mulvaney and his friend, Marc, who wanted to learn to make Mexican food and came to consult my cookery books. The boys ended up using tortillas as frisbees in my kitchen. Both of them have children and restaurants of their own now.

Frankie, Gene and I often take their children and various of their friends to a wonderful spot we call "The Magic Place." We found it one day quite by accident while looking for somewhere to picnic. It was a holiday, we were in a large woodland that had picnic tables at intervals along the narrow winding road and all of them were full, so we just kept going. Finally, ready to give up, we pulled into what we thought was a turning area and saw a few tables – all empty – and amazingly beyond some boulders a tiny, beautiful lake with a waterfall. Except for the fact that it is not on any map, we still can't imagine why no one was there, and to this day we rarely encounter anyone else (and even when we do they are never using the picnic tables). The lake is wonderful to swim in, and we've discovered that unless the stream above is running too swiftly the waterfall flows into a little pool that has become our own Jacuzzi. Between swims we have a picnic that usually includes potato salad – but only for us adults – and oddly enough, none of the Irish children will have anything to do with it.

I was nearly touched to tears one evening when two small boys I had never seen before knocked on our door with a gift of freshly caught mackerel. Another favorite incident involving children with fish is one of the times I tried to purchase smoked salmon. Some of the best smoked salmon we've ever had is done locally by Chris, but unlike the obliging Cyril, Chris has no telephone and can be elusive. This time it seemed the only way to order his product was to meet the school bus and give a written request to more than one of his several offspring with a prayer that they wouldn't forget to pass it on to their dad. It worked but probably only because I elected to meet the school bus at the end of the day rather than in the morning.

Although he arrives in a shiny red car and not an old wagon, I like to think that the man who peddles fish around these out-of-the-way places is a page out of time as well. I never know when to expect him. It can be at any hour or any day. I was already in bed one night, when Richard saw him coming through the gate with lobsters. Quite often, after not seeing him for some while, we have met on our boreen when I'm returning from the fish shop in town, and though he never seems perturbed if I don't need anything, I do try to encourage his enterprise and order something for a specific date. I rarely get what I asked for, however, and usually not on the specified day, but he might bring a substitute of his choice the following week. If that happens to be cod or hake, I will buy a whole one, cut it into fillets, give the skin to the gulls, save some bits for the cats, and use the rest of the trimmings to make Thai fish cakes which I then freeze.

Thai Fish Cakes

1 lb. ground cod or hake

1 egg

$^1/_2$ tablespoon red Thai curry paste

6 Kaffir lime leaves, ground*

2 tablespoons Thai fish sauce

$^3/_4$ lb. green beans, thinly sliced

oil for deep frying

Thoroughly mix together the cod, egg, red curry paste, lime leaves and fish sauce. Stir in the beans, form the mixture into balls using a rounded tablespoon for each one and then flatten the balls into cakes. Deep-fry the cakes in 350°–375° oil for about $1^1/_2$–2 minutes, turning, until they are light brown. Serve them with Cucumber Mint Sauce. Makes about 35 cakes.
* In Thailand they shred the leaves very finely, but I have found it easier to grind them in a spice mill.

Cucumber Mint Sauce

$^1/_2$ **cup white vinegar**

$^1/_4$ **cup water**

$^1/_4$ **cup sugar**

2 teaspoons Thai fish sauce

1 teaspoon red chili paste

1 medium cucumber, peeled, seeded and chopped

2 tablespoons chopped fresh mint

Bring the vinegar, water, sugar, fish sauce and chili paste to a boil, stirring to dissolve the sugar. Cool and stir in the cucumber and mint.

Over the years Richard and I have been fortunate enough to dine in many of the world's very best restaurants, and each time we have found ourselves comparing them with our favorite spots in Ireland, where the meals are excellent and the locale and ambience unbeatable. Because our son Kevin is a chef and we have always had many friends in the food business (all of whom say that what they appreciate most on an evening out is that they don't have to cook it themselves), I should know better than to get myself into a dither when entertaining them. Still it was really daunting the first time I had four couples who own very good restaurants – and nearly all of them are chefs as well – to dinner at the same time. It was also one of the few occasions (thank God) when I had a serious and irretrievable culinary disaster before a dinner party.

For this dinner I wanted colors in the appetizer to be complementary with the centerpiece and dishes, and decided on a monkfish and vegetable terrine that I'd successfully experimented with. The other times I'd made this terrine I'd done it a day ahead and sliced it about an hour before serving. This time I made it a day in advance as usual, but luckily sliced it early on the day. It looked fine, it didn't smell funny, but for some reason I tasted it. It TASTED funny. The monkfish had gone off. The whole thing went onto the compost, where it made a colorful

Lillian and Larry
Beard with
Richard at
Healy Pass

topping which intrigued a couple of magpies until the cats came along and demolished the lot.

The replacement did not particularly tie in with the table setting. I had quite a few onions that were sprouting and used the sprouts to make a soup that I garnished with chive flowers – which turned out to be a happy choice. When we sat down, one of the guests remarked that he had been hoping for a cold soup on this hot evening. Strangely, although they all commented how good it was, no one was able to guess just what was in the soup – the majority vote went to asparagus.

Sprouted Onion Soup

2 shallots, chopped

a little vegetable oil

12–14 well-sprouted onions, green parts only, roughly chopped

6 pints chicken stock

cream

Sauté the shallots in a little oil until just softened, add the onions, cover and cook over very low heat for 10 minutes. Add the chicken stock and simmer for 40 minutes to one hour. Cool and puree very thoroughly. Add some cream but not too much. Serves 10.

When the vegetable produce is too much for our own use, we give a lot away, mainly to those friends with heavy overhead costs of running restaurants. Richard says he wonders how many people bring the salad with them when they go to a restaurant and then pay for it. At the end of one season, when we went to dinner at Blairs Cove we took the usual lettuces, herbs, and the even heftier than normal remainder of our summer squashes to Philippe and Sabine.

It must seem a little strange to other diners, but rather than going around to the kitchen, it's easier to take the basketful of vegetables in with us when we arrive. This particular offering, however, was so heavy that Philippe sent one of his staff out to collect it from the car. He apparently didn't shut the boot tightly and when we drove away the rattling was driving me crazy, so before we turned onto the main road I insisted on getting out to fix it – and fell into a cattle grid. It is no secret that in spite of my heritage I have gained a deserved reputation for being a general klutz. Over the years, friends and family have grown accustomed to my everyday mishaps, so when I yelped, laughed and said not to worry, Richard didn't cut the motor or get out until he looked in the rearview mirror and saw a lady jump from the car following us and come to my assistance. He had inadvertently stopped partly on the grid and, of course, when I went to shut the hatch in the dark, my foot went through and my left leg slid down between the bars up to the knee. Fortunately the rest of our party, the rotten Collins sisters, were ahead of us. They said that due to paralytic laughter, they would have been useless to help. I knew I was all right, but Richard was truly worried that I might have been seriously injured, and he was baffled that although I ruined good white silk trousers, my main relief was that I hadn't lost my sandal.

With its elegant chandelier hanging from the high ceiling of a spacious, lovely room that once was a stable, one would never expect Blairs Cove to be located where it is, hidden away in the countryside overlooking the bay. We wonder how many people have to coax steers out of the way before they can proceed up the long drive to the restaurant, or while chatting with Maureen O'Hara at the next table are watched by a mare and her foal with their noses pressed against the window.

One of our favorite of so many good times at this great restaurant was an evening when tables were put together to accommodate a large group. It turned out to be a surprise birthday party and many of us in the dining room applauded the arrival of the guest of honor, a slim, dapper gentleman. Some Americans, who obviously thought he must be someone they should recognize, asked who he was. I was delighted to answer that he was Justin, the butcher from Bantry, of course.

Blairs Cove Fillet of Salmon with Horseradish Crust

For crust:	3 oz. butter
2 tablespoons horseradish	salt and pepper
6 oz. smoked salmon or marinated salmon	
$2^1/_2$ cups white bread crumbs	5 salmon fillets
juice of 1 lemon	white wine and fish stock

In a processor mix all the crust ingredients to a firm dough. If it is too soft, add a bit more bread. (Dough will keep in the fridge for several days.) Roll the dough out as thin as possible, cut it into pieces the size of the salmon fillets, and crisscross with a sharp knife. Lay the dough on top of the fillets and put them into an ovenproof dish with a bit of white wine and fish stock, and bake at 400° for about 10 minutes. Before serving, pass under a broiler to brown the crust. Serve with Hollandaise sauce or beurre blanc.

Whatever leftovers the cats won't eat go onto the compost heap, where they are stolen by the local birds – notably Bubba, a seagull who Richard can now feed by hand, and his more timid lady, whom we've named Bubbette. We've become so fond of them that I'm afraid I don't always offer just leftovers. I once bought a beef heart which Richard valiantly cut up and served onto the roof from the bedroom window (but refused to do ever again), and if I haven't anything else I've been known to open a can of cat food or defrost something I think may have been in the freezer too long. Now when we dine out, the staff ask if we want a gull or a kitty bag. Burvill the Welshman and his lovely, dotty Chrissy, who have the excellent and very pretty Restaurant in Blue, find it extremely funny that Bubba and Bubbette sit on our chimney all day waiting for a handout. When he rang to say he was in the vicinity and asked if I could spare any fennel, Burvill could hear them screaming at some other birds trying to approach their personal private buffet and I explained that their food was nearly gone. He offered to give us replenishment when he could and has since been freezing a supply of salmon and other fish skins to bring down to us, and I reward him with watercress, dill, lettuce and coriander as well as fennel. Fair exchange, I think, for Bubbette's feast.

Burvill's Quail Stuffed with an Olive Paté on a Bed of Fried Spring Greens

$^1/_2$ lb. fresh olives, stoned	olive oil
$2^1/_2$ oz. foie gras	$^1/_2$ cup marsala
some bread crumbs soaked in a little olive oil	$^1/_8$ cup port wine
4 small quails	1 cup good chicken stock
some cape gooseberries or grapes	some finely shredded spring greens
8 garlic cloves, not skinned	oil for deep frying

Take the olives, foie gras, and bread crumbs and put them all into a processor until blended. Stuff the mixture into each of the quails along with the gooseberries or grapes. Truss the birds, and place them on a baking tray with the garlic cloves in between. Bake the quails in a 375° oven, basting with a little olive oil, for about 20 minutes, until they are nice and golden.
For the sauce, take a good-bottomed pan and pour in the marsala and the port wine, bring to a boil, and flame to burn off the excess alcohol. Now add the chicken stock and season to your taste. Reduce the sauce. Take the finely shredded greens and throw into hot oil, and take out as soon as the oil stops sizzling.
Place greens on a hot plate, and arrange the quails on top with the garlic cloves on either side. Now take the reduced sauce, pour over and serve.
This sauce is clear but full of flavor. Serves 2.

Even though cooking has become big business all over the world, many people, recalling the days of boiled, mashed and French fried potatoes served together with limp, gray cabbage and soggy brown string beans, are still surprised to find that Ireland now has so many truly good places to eat. Understandably surprising, however, is that we have Kai's superb Japanese restaurant, Shiro, tranquilly set out in the countryside among gardens and trees, overlooking the sea.

As with many of the other restaurant owners, we are friends with Kai and Werner. The others, however, don't try to foist kittens on you after dinner. Believing that two cats were enough for any household, we had always resisted until one evening at Shiro with our American guests, Larry and Tomo Billman. We wanted to give little Tomo a taste of Japan in Ireland, which she said was sensational, and both ladies were grateful for the chance to speak their first language for a while once more. Kai knew we had lost our beloved old ginger cat, George, after seventeen years, and since we were the only people left in the restaurant, she struck while the iron was hot, and brought out a basket full of kittens after dessert. No resisting this time – we NEEDED a new cat. The one we chose seemed to dance around the others, and since Larry and Tomo had both been dancers, we called him Larry, too. The following week I went back to bring him home, and he has become the most loving cat I've ever known. I don't know about his brothers and sisters but my Larry still likes the taste of soy sauce.

While Burvill brings fish skins to our seagulls, Annie takes the leftovers (including mussels in garlic butter) from her restaurant to feed her brother's pigs.

Annie is a warmhearted, gregarious, pretty woman who dated our son Tyler when they were in boarding school together. Her restaurant, a tiny little place simply called "Annie's," has been written up all over the country and on the Continent and is seldom empty unless Annie is having a baby and closes for a while. She has a wine license, but everyone goes across the street for drinks first at the Levis (pronounced Levvis or Leevis but not like the jeans) sisters' pub before dinner. Annie brings the menus, takes orders and comes to fetch you from there.

Annie's Baked Avocado with Crab Meat:

"Chunks of avocado on top of crab meat mixed with a béchamel sauce, topped with Gubbeen cheese (or another mature cheese), baked in the oven for about ten minutes and then flashed under the grill [broiler] before serving."

Nell and Julia Levis, in their eighties, were born in the house and have lived above the pub-cum-shop their entire lives. Though spinsters, they are still good looking, and must have been very pretty as girls. Nell has close-cropped white hair, wears sneakers and usually vivid ski sweaters, but we have seen her in a Los Angeles Lakers sweatshirt and Nikes. Julia catches her long, still-auburn hair up in a knot held by a Spanish-type tortoise comb and calls Richard "Boyeen" (Irish vernacular for "boy"). Nell and Julia often holiday in Florida, but they feel they really don't have to travel because the world finds its way to them. And it does.

Julia didn't know who he was until later, but one afternoon she had a long chat at the bar with Kevin Costner, and, during one of his visits to the area when he was still prime minister, Garret Fitzgerald dined at Annie's while his bodyguards waited at Nell and Julia's pub. By the time he finished his meal, the bodyguards were supposedly so looped the P.M. had to drive them home. That might be blarney, but after living in this magical country for so long a time, I find another of my most favorite things is the fact that, basically, all Irish stories are true.

**Nell and Julia
pulling pints**

On the subject of pubs, although my father didn't drink much, his favorite was a bourbon Old Fashioned which my mother taught me to make when I was a little girl and, although I never mixed one for him at Levis's, I have done so or shown the publican how at a bar in Lismore and others around Ireland.

I suppose my final recipe shouldn't be for a cocktail, but making my father's drink was one of my favorite things and it seems right to include it.

My father with his Old Fashioned

F. A.'s Old Fashioned

Angostura bitters

1 sugar cube

soda water

2 oz. bourbon

ice

1 maraschino cherry and a little of its syrup

half an orange slice

In an Old Fashioned glass sprinkle about 6 drops of bitters on the sugar cube and add soda water to just cover. Crush the cube with a wooden pestle, add bourbon, ice, a scant teaspoon of cherry syrup and stir. Spear orange and cherry on a toothpick, put them in the glass and top up with a dash more soda.

Liquid Measures

American	Fluid Ounces	Irish/British	Metric
1 teaspoon	$1/8$ fl. oz.	1 teaspoon	5 milliliters
2 teaspoons	$1/4$ fl. oz.	1 dessertspoon	10 ml.
1 tablespoon	$1/2$ fl. oz.	1 tablespoon	15 ml.
2 tablespoons	1 fl. oz.	2 tablespoons	30 ml.
$1/4$ cup	2 fl. oz.	4 tablespoons	56 ml.
$1/3$ cup	$2 2/3$ fl. oz.		80 ml.
$1/2$ cup	4 fl. oz.		110 ml.
$2/3$ cup	5 fl. oz.	$1/4$ pint	140 ml.
$3/4$ cup	6 fl. oz.		170 ml.
1 cup	8 fl. oz.		225 ml.
$1 1/4$ cups	10 fl. oz.	1 cup/$1/2$ pint	280 ml.
2 cups/1 pint	16 fl. oz.		450 ml.
$2 1/2$ cups	20 fl. oz.	2 cups/1 pint	560 ml.
3 cups	24 fl. oz.		675 ml.

Solid Measures

American/ Irish/British	Metric
1 oz.	25 grams
$3 1/2$ oz.	100 g.
4 oz./$1/4$ lb.	110 g.
5 oz.	150 g.
6 oz.	175 g.
7 oz.	200 g.
8 oz./$1/2$ lb.	225 g.
9 oz.	250 g.
10 oz.	275 g.
12 oz./$3/4$ lb.	350 g.
16 oz./1 lb.	450 g.
$1 1/2$ lbs.	675 g.
2 lbs.	900 g.
$2 1/4$ lbs.	1000 g./1 kilogram

Oven Temperatures

American/ Fahrenheit	Gas Mark	Celsius
225°	$1/4$	110°
250°	$1/2$	130°
275°	1	140°
300°	2	150°
325°	3	170°
350°	4	180°
375°	5	190°
400°	6	200°
425°	7	220°
450°	8	230°
475°	9	240°

For measuring dry ingredients in cups, American cups are roughly equivalent to a large level teacup.

★*All of the recipes in this book use American measurements.*